FOCUSED ON THE ONE

Women's Bible Study Series

3:16

A Guided Journal Through All the Books of the Bible That Have a Chapter 3, Verse 16

JENNIFER GALVAN

CROSSROADS PUBLISHERS

3:16

A Guided Journal Through all the Books of the Bible That Have a Chapter 3, Verse 16

Library of Congress Control Number: 2024927493

ISBN: 979-8-9913821-4-4

Published By CrossRoads Publishers, Lakewood, California

Contents

INTRODUCTION

> "For God so loved the world, that He gave His only begotten Son, that whosoever believeth in Him should not perish, but have everlasting life."
>
> John 3:16 KJV

John 3:16 is the most famous verse in the Bible. It is proof of God's love for each and every one of us and has been the conduit that has led a great many people to a saving knowledge of Him.

Welcome to *3:16*, an interactive Bible study journal designed for women. While John 3:16 may have been one of the first verses you memorized, and played a significant role in your relationship with Christ, have you ever considered the insights God has to share with you through all the other 3:16s in the Bible?

This journal will guide you through each book of the Bible that contains a chapter 3, verse 16, inviting you to explore the depth and richness of these verses as you deepen your faith and understanding of God's word.

There are 49 Books of the Bible that contain a 3:16, and many of these speak directly to women or are verses that apply to the challenges that women face. It is my hope that as you study the 3:16s of the Bible that God will draw you into a closer relationship with Him and you will find strength from these verses.

I am Jennifer Galvan, a pastor's wife, author, speaker and advocate for helping people creatively experience God's word. I grew up attending church in my small town and came to know the Lord as my personal Savior at age 10. At age 18, I headed off for University and it was at this time that my interest in studying the Word of God and spending time in prayer truly began to grow.

The inspiration for 3:16 came on a flight from Tennessee to California. I came across John 3:16 and wondered if 3:16 in the other gospels were similar to John 3:16 (spoiler alert: they are not). This led to a 4 hour flight of studying the 3:16's of the Bible.

Get ready to dig into your Bible in a brand new way. Choosing one verse from each book of the Bible is not a typical way to study the Bible. When studying an individual verse, it is important to read the verse carefully so you can take in the meaning of every word. However, it is even more important to understand the context that verse came from. The Biblical context surrounding a verse can completely change its meaning from what it seems to be when the verse stands alone. This is why you should always read the context verses before and/or after your focus verse so you will truly understand the meaning God gave to that verse.

God has gifted women with creative minds, and this Bible study journal is designed with that in mind. In 3:16 you will find Bible Journaling opportunities, with many different activities which will give you the ability to make this book your own. You may want to pick up a set of colored pencils and stickers to use as you complete this journal as it is intended to be decorated in your own personal style.

When God knit you together in the womb, He knew that you would pick up this journal, and He has something to say to you as you study the 3:16s of His word.

You can jump right in or turn to the, "*Ways to Use this 3:16 Bible Study Journal*" in the back pages of this book for a detailed outline of how to utilize this Bible Study to best suit your needs.

ACKNOWLEDGMENTS

I would like to write 136 words to say thank you to those who have helped bring this to life.

Kathy, my fearless editor and publisher whose talent continues to astound me. Abel, my supportive husband and the best Pastor I have ever known. Joy, it is a privilege to watch you grow in your faith each and every day. My parents, whose Godly example gave me a solid foundation in Christ and allowed me to express my creativity in writing. Those who are family by blood and by choice. Pastors that have shared the word of God with me for the last fifty one years, your ministry continues to shape and influence my Christian journey. Finally, to those of you who counted every one of these words just to see if there actually were 136.

How to Use this Journal

For every 3:16 you will be given:

3:16 Verse:

There are forty-nine 3:16s in the Bible. Since every chapter is a 3:16, this header will also give you the Book of the Bible and translation used for each individual 3:16 in this book.

Genesis 3:16 NLT

We will start with Genesis 3:16 and continue in order through Revelation 3:16. Every 3:16 is its own chapter and is designed to stand alone.

Biblical Context:

Every verse in the Bible has a context that it is set in. Without the context, it is nearly impossible to grasp the full meaning of the verse and what it truly says.

3:16 BIBLICAL Context

This Biblical Context is a timeline that will give you enough information regarding the context to allow you to understand what is being discussed in the 3:16. It will also have a verse notation for each point in the timeline, in case you would like to read that section for yourself. You will want to refer to your Bible for the full scope of the Biblical Content.

Exploring 3:16:

This section will allow for a deeper look at the passage.

If the 3:16 you are studying has a direct or contextual correlation to John 3:16, that correlation will also be discussed in this section.

3:16 Reflect & Connect:

The Reflect & Connect section focuses on you.

It is here to give you an opportunity to reflect on what you have just learned and connect it to your life. Sometimes it may prompt you to pray for something, draw, journal, or do something to express your creativity. Reflect & Connect allows your brain to connect with the verse, strengthening your knowledge of the Bible and deepening your faith.

Closing Prayer:

This last section in the chapter is dedicated to a time of prayer.

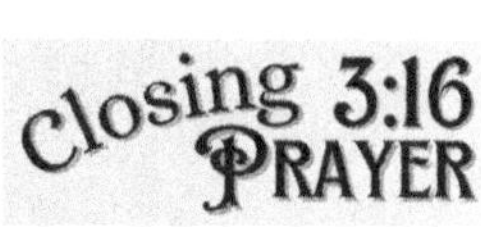

Each prayer will begin with an opening such as "Heavenly Father". There are many ways to begin a prayer, so use the one that best fits your needs.

Each prayer will close with "in Jesus' name I pray, Amen". Again, there are many ways to end a time in prayer, so please use the one that best shows your adoration to the Lord.

Throughout the prayer, there may be blank lines to give you an opportunity to pray for specific things or people. When you come across these blanks, try to be open to who or what the Lord wants you to pray for or about. Feel free to fill in the blanks if there is room, however, please know that it is not a requirement, rather an opportunity for God to bring someone or something to your mind.

The prayer listed is a guide to draw you into communication with God. Feel free to use any parts of the prayer that suit you, however, don't be limited by the words written in this section. Pray as God leads you before you end your Closing Prayer.

Example:

Heavenly Father,

I thank you for guiding me to this study and I ask that you give me the determination to complete all the 3:16s in Your word. As I begin, I know that ______________ has been a distraction in my life and I ask that You work in my life to help me be successful in learning more about You. As I close this time with You, I want to thank You for ______________

In Jesus' name I pray,

Amen

Genesis 3:16 NLT

Then He said to the woman, "I will sharpen the pain of your pregnancy, and in pain you will give birth. And you will desire to control your husband, but he will rule over you."

Genesis 3:16 NLT

3:16 Biblical Context

Timeline of Genesis 3:1-24

✧ **Genesis 3:1** – The serpent asks the woman a leading question about eating from the trees in the Garden of Eden.

✧ **Genesis 3:2-3** – The woman answers the question in a way that tells us that she knows about God's command to not eat the fruit from the tree of the knowledge of good and evil.

✧ **Genesis 3:4-5** – The serpent creates doubt and lies to the woman, "You won't die! ...your eyes will be opened...and you will be like God, knowing both good and evil."

✧ **Genesis 3:6** – The woman is convinced. She and the man eat the fruit from the tree of the knowledge of good and evil.

✧ **Genesis 3:7-8** – As soon as they eat the fruit they are convicted. They hide from God.

✧ **Genesis 3:9-13** – God comes looking for them and they discuss what the man and woman did.

✧ **Genesis 3:14-19** – God curses the serpent, the woman, and the man.

✧ **Genesis 3:20-24** – Adam & Eve are named. God provides animal skin clothing for them. Then God banishes them from the Garden of Eden.

EXPLORING Genesis 3:16

From the beginning of the Bible, God has spoken to women. In a society where women were not given equal rights, God made sure that His word included words spoken directly to women. In Genesis 3:16 we see the consequences of sin that still apply directly to women today.

The first part of Genesis 3:16 tells us that God is about to make a direct statement to women:

"*Then He said to the woman,*"

The second is a curse regarding sin, that directly applies to something that only happens to women:

"*I will sharpen the pain of your pregnancy, and in pain you will give birth.*"

The last is a statement to women about who will be in charge from then on:

" *And you will desire to control your husband, but he will rule over you.*"

Up to this point in human history, God has been the one in charge. He created them, provided a place for them to live, food for them to eat, a rule to follow, and told them the ultimate consequence of breaking that rule. In all their time together God showed Himself to be benevolent and loving. They had the closest relationship with God that any of us will ever experience this side of heaven.

However, their disobedience did a lot more than tell God that they were no longer willing to let Him rule over them. Their disobedience separated them from God and let sin into the world.

Fortunately for the world, even in that separation, He provided for Adam & Eve back then, just as He provides for us today.

John 3:16 Correlation: The statement the serpent made to Eve was true. Eve did not die when she ate the fruit, and her eyes were opened to the knowledge of both good and evil. However, the serpent also lied. Eve did die. Not immediately, but had she obeyed, Eve would still be alive today.

Sin always separates us from God. And though we see what happened with Eve, we still fall into the trappings of sin, and find that, just like Eve, sin separates us from God.

Death was the ultimate consequence of their disobedience. A consequence that met its match in God's provision for us. Jesus came to earth to live amongst us and the promise of John 3:16 was fulfilled when His willing sacrifice on the cross broke the curse and bridged our separation from God, creating a way for us to get back into permanent fellowship with God.

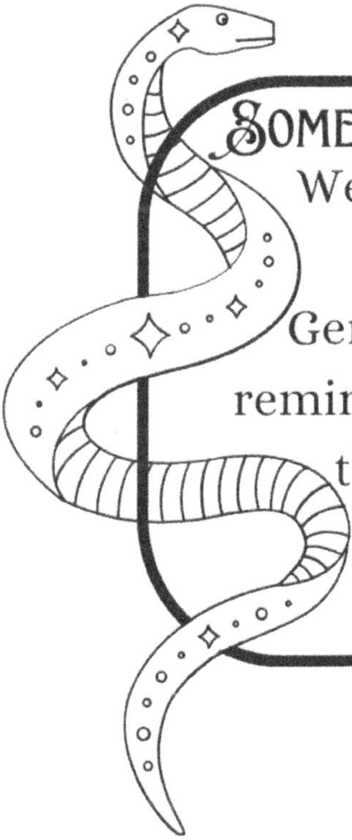

Something to Think About:

We as women like to be in the know. God put Genesis 3:16 in His word to remind us to be careful of those things that can lead us off of God's chosen path for us.

3:16 Reflect & Connect

As you begin this Bible study journal, think about a time when God has told you something directly through His word and you did not follow through with it. Write down a reminder of how that situation played out in your life. It may be hard to write down that failure, but looking back on our lives and owning our mistakes gives us clarity about how to move forward and not make similar mistakes in the future.

Closing 3:16 Prayer

Heavenly Father,

I thank You for guiding me to this study and I ask that You give me the determination to complete all the 3:16s in Your word. As I begin, I know that _______________ has been a distraction in my life and I ask that You work in my life to help me be successful in learning more about You. As I close this first chapter, I want to thank You for ______________.

In Jesus' name I pray,
Amen

Exodus 3:16 NLT

"Now go and call together all the elders of Israel. Tell them, 'Yahweh, the God of your ancestors—the God of Abraham, Isaac, and Jacob—has appeared to me. He told me, "I have been watching closely, and I see how the Egyptians are treating you,

Exodus 3:16 NLT

3:16 Biblical Context

Timeline of Exodus 3-4

- ✧ **Exodus 3:1-4:17** – God calls Moses and talks to him from a burning bush.
- ✧ **Exodus 3: 7-11** – God tells Moses to go to Pharaoh & Moses protests.
- ✧ **Exodus 3:12-13** – God promises Moses a sign that He will be with him & Moses protests again.
- ✧ **Exodus 3:14- 4:1** – God tells Moses exactly what He wants him to do and why & Moses protests yet again.
- ✧ **Exodus 4:2-10** – God gets bold and uses signs to get Moses's attention: Moses's staff turned into a snake & Moses places his hand inside his cloak and when he pulls his hand back out it is covered with a skin disease & Moses still protests that he does not speak well.
- ✧ **Exodus 4:11-13** – God promises to help Moses and tells him to go again & Moses pleads with God to send anyone else.
- ✧ **Exodus 4:14-31** – God finally gets angry and almost kills him but Moses' wife intervenes on his behalf and saves Moses' life.

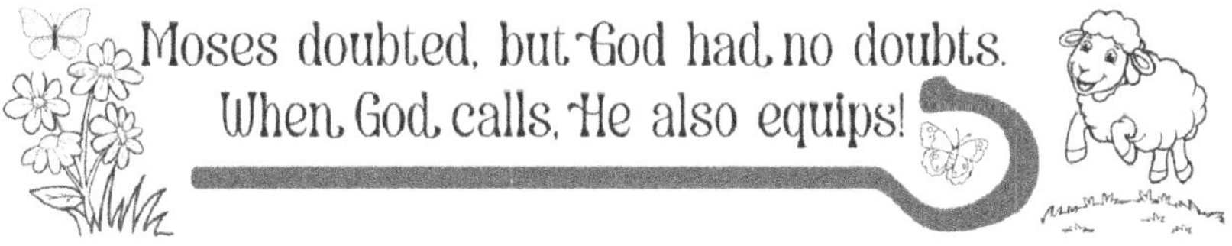

EXPLORING Exodus 3:16

It all started with a burning bush. Not just any burning bush, but a burning bush that was not being consumed. God talked to Moses as he stood at this burning bush.

One would think that would have been a WOW moment for Moses. God was speaking to him out of a burning bush! Moses started out respectful and obedient, removing his sandals because it was holy ground, and once Moses understood that it was God talking to him, he was afraid to look at God, so he covered his face. The God of all creation... The God of Abraham, Isaac, and Jacob, who was talking to him from a burning bush, told Moses to help Him set His people free, and Moses argued with Him.

Fortunately, God's intervention on the Israelites behalf was not withdrawn due to Moses' protests. Moses finally conceded to God's request and led His people out of Egypt, freeing the Israelites from slavery.

John 3:16 Correlation: God intervened on the Israelites behalf to set them free from slavery. Just as Jesus intervened on the world's behalf to set us free from our slavery to sin.

SOMETHING TO THINK ABOUT:

Exodus 3:16 is a reminder that God hears our cries and moves at His perfect time.

In your Egypt, are you waiting patiently for Him, or trying to rush the process?

3:16 Reflect & Connect

God has put people in your life that you intervene on behalf of. Whether this is a spouse, a child, a friend, or someone else entirely, write the name of that person or those people here and spend time praying for them.

____

____

Now take some time to consider how God used Moses, flawed as he was, to work in the lives of the Israelites, to lead them and be the conduit for understanding God's will. Look back at the name(s) you wrote, and write a prayer asking God to use you in the lives of those whom He has called you to minister to.

____

____

____

____

____

Closing 3:16 Prayer

Heavenly Father,

You have brought ______________ to my mind. Lord, I want to thank You for them and I know that You love them more than I do. I ask You to use me to work in their life. Lord, I want to be open to what You might have me do, so I ask that You prepare me to be a support and give me the knowledge to intervene in whatever situation this person needs help with.

In Jesus' name I pray.
Amen

Leviticus 3:16 NLT

And the priest will burn them on the altar. It is a special gift of food, a pleasing aroma to the Lord. "All the fat belongs to the Lord".

Leviticus 3:16 NLT

3:16 Biblical Context

Timeline of Leviticus 3:1-17

- **Leviticus 3:1-16** – Tells the person presenting an animal as their peace offering, what they need to do to make the offering pleasing to the Lord.
- **Leviticus 3:17** – Is a permanent law for the Israelites that must be observed from generation to generation wherever they live, telling them that they *must never eat any fat or blood.*

Exploring Leviticus 3:16

Leviticus 3 gives us a look at the way peace offerings were made in the Bible. This verse specifically speaks about peace or fellowship offerings. A fellowship offering was an offering that was given after a sin or atonement offering. It expressed thankfulness that the worshiper's relationship with God had been healed and their fellowship with God had been restored.

Now, let's talk about that second sentence in Leviticus 3:16,

"All the fat belongs to the Lord."

It's okay if you smiled when you read that—the Bible literally says, "all the fat belongs to the Lord."

Ladies, we often struggle with our bodies, and although this verse is talking about the part of an animal that is sacrificed, it can be a reminder that just as the Israelites were called to honor God with their sacrifices, we can honor Him by loving and accepting the bodies He has given us.

John 3:16 Correlation: Think about the concept of sacrificial offerings restoring the relationship between humanity and God. The focus is on the sacrifice as a means to bridge the gap caused by sin.

John 3:16, presents Jesus as the ultimate and final sacrifice. Jesus' death on the cross fulfills the Old Testament system of sacrifices and offers eternal reconciliation between God and humanity.

3:16 Reflect & Connect

Think about how this 3:16 talks about the sacrifice being a pleasing aroma to the Lord and spend some time writing down areas in your life that need to be a pleasing aroma to God. Below are topics to get you started:

✦ Forgiveness for any sin you have committed.

✦ Peace in areas of your life that are not always peaceful.

✦ Ask God to reveal to you areas of your life that you are carrying guilt and release those to God.

Closing 3:16 Prayer

Heavenly Father,

I want to be a pleasing aroma to You in all that I do. God, please work in my life in the areas I have written above. Lord, I ask that You bring this study to my mind this week to remind me of the __________ that I am working on.

In Jesus' name I pray,

Amen

Numbers 3:16 NLT

So Moses listed them, just as the Lord had commanded.

Numbers 3:16 NLT

3:16 Biblical Context

Timeline of Numbers 3:5-39

- **Numbers 3:5-13** – God instructs Moses to call the tribe of Levi to serve the community, performing sacred duties in and around the Tabernacle, and maintaining the Tabernacle.
- **Numbers 3:14-16** – God instructs Moses to list the male members of the tribe of Levi by their families and clans.
- **Numbers 3:17-39** – This is the list of the Levites, who numbered 22,000, and their responsibilities for the community and the Tabernacle.

Exploring Numbers 3:16

This 3:16 was a command from the Lord to Moses when he was in the wilderness of Sanai. The Lord asked Moses to list the name of every man in the tribe of Levi which registered all males of one month and older as Levites. When all was said and done, the Levite clans numbered 22,000 males one month or older.

John 3:16 Correlation: Ponder God's intentional care and provision for His people. Ensuring that every member of the tribe of Levi was counted in this census shows God's deliberate preparation and organization to ensure His people had a way to come into His presence, through the priestly system He established with the clans of Levi.

While the tribe of Levites were mediators in the Old Covenant, Jesus became the ultimate mediator in the New Covenant, making direct access to God available to everyone through their belief in Him.

God's intentional and personal care for each of us shows in this passage. Just as God called the Levites to serve and mediate for the Israelites, He has uniquely called and equipped each of us with gifts to serve in ways that nurture our families, communities and churches. God's love, demonstrated so powerfully in John 3:16, reminds us that He cherishes each individual. His plan to give Jesus as our eternal mediator means we are not just set apart for service, but also deeply loved and cared for.

3:16 Reflect & Connect

As women, we are invited to live out God's love daily, using our unique roles to reflect God's intentional care, and we can be assured that our contributions matter to God. Like the Levites, we are called to bring God's presence into every aspect of our lives.

Take a moment to write down all the Men in your tribe. Spouse, children, extended family members. Once you have your list, move to the Closing Prayer to begin praying for the tribe of men God has placed in your life.

Closing 3:16 Prayer

Heavenly Father,

I lift up the men in my tribe to You now. I pray for __________ specifically as he needs Your guidance in ___________. I pray for ___________ as he is dealing with ___________ in his life. Lord, I praise You for giving me the men in my life and I ask that You bring them to my mind this week so I can continue to lift them in prayer.

In Jesus' name I pray,

Amen

Deuteronomy 3:16 NLT

But I also gave part of Gilead to the tribes of Reuben and Gad. The area I gave them extended from the middle of the Arnon Gorge in the south to the Jabbok River on the Ammonite frontier.

Deuteronomy 3:16 NLT

3:16 Biblical Context

Timeline of Deuteronomy 3:1-11, 3:16-29

- **Deuteronomy 3:1-7** – Moses recounts to the Israelites their victories in battle, even in the face of challenging circumstances and formidable foes.
- **Deuteronomy 3:8-11** – Moses reminds his people how they had been able to take possession of the land, down to the last survivor, King Og who is listed as a commanding presence.
- **Deuteronomy 3:16-22** – Moses commands the tribes to help conquer the land on the western side of the Jordan River that God has promised them before they can return to their allotted territory.
- **Deuteronomy 3:23-29** – Moses recalled how he pled with God to let him enter the promised land. God denied his request but told Moses to go to the peak of the mountain to view the promised land.

Exploring Deuteronomy 3:16

Deuteronomy is the final book of the Pentateuch (the name for the first 5 books of the Bible, also known by the Jews as the Torah). Moses is prominently featured in this book through a series of speeches to the Israelites. And throughout it all we see Moses in both the highs and lows of his faithfulness to God.

Deuteronomy 3 gives us a look at one aspect of what God had assigned Moses to do. He was given the task of dividing the land between the tribes. Moses also had to command the fighting men of those tribes to continue to help the rest of the tribes of Israel claim the entirety of the promised land before they could come back and settle on their chosen land. Deuteronomy 5 includes Moses' recap of the 10 Commandments and Deuteronomy 34 ends with Moses' death just outside of the promised land.

John 3:16 Correlation: In Deuteronomy 3:16, God directs Moses to divide the land, assigning territories east of the Jordan to the tribes of Reuben and Gad. This distribution is part of God's promise to provide a secure place for his people, establishing them in safety with His provision.

John 3:16, on a larger scale, shows us the ultimate fulfillment of God's promise through Jesus, whose death, burial, and resurrection provides those who believe in Him, eternal life.

While Deuteronomy shows God's caring for His people by securing their physical inheritance, John 3:16 offers the assurance of an eternal inheritance through Christ. God cares for His people through both His promises and His protection.

3:16 Reflect & Connect

Spend some time reading Deuteronomy 3-5. While you are reading, jot down some things that catch your attention in these chapters.

Read the 10 Commandments out loud. Write them down on, "The 10 Commitments" tablets provided, and make a commitment to memorize them.

The 10 Commandments

Closing 3:16 Prayer

Heavenly Father,

You have given me the 10 Commandments as a guide for my life, I pray them to You now.

1. You have commanded that I have no other god but You. Lord, I confess that I tend to put _________ in front of You and I ask forgiveness for that. Lord, it is my prayer that I can keep You first in my life.

2. You have commanded that I not make an idol of any kind. Lord, I understand that there are many things in my life that I can make idols out of, like my job, money, or even people I admire. I ask Lord that You help me to keep my eyes focused on You so that nothing else has a chance to become an idol in my life.

3. You have commanded that I must not misuse the name of the Lord my God. Your name is Holy and I ask forgiveness for times that I have not used Your name in Holy ways. I ask that You remind me to honor Your name in every word that comes from

my mouth.

4. You have commanded me to observe the Sabbath day by keeping it holy. Lord You created the earth in 6 days and then You rested on the 7th day. God I make a commitment to follow Your example and take a day of rest. Heavenly Father, I will use the Sabbath to rest in You.

5. You have commanded me to honor my father and mother. Lord, You have given me the father and mother You chose.

   a. *If your parents are alive* – I pray for ____________ today that You will work in their lives today in the following ways ________________.

   b. *If your parents are no longer alive* – Heavenly Father I thank You for the parents You gave me. Lord, there are times I miss them greatly and I pray You will be close to me during those times.

   c. *If you do not have a healthy relationship with your parents* – Lord, my relationship with my parents was not perfect and there were times when I did not understand why. God I bring those things to you now and ask for healing for the unhealed hurt present in my relationship with my parents.

6. You have commanded me to not commit murder. God You have created everyone on earth and I pray that I will respect the sanctity of human life.

7. You have commanded me to not commit adultery. God You have been clear how You expect my relationships to honor You.

   a. *For those who are unmarried* – I pray that You will help me to be chaste and keep my eyes focused on You.

   b. *For those who are married* – Lord, thank You for the spouse You have blessed me with. I ask that You allow me to remain faithful to my spouse and be patient and forgiving with them.

8. You have commanded me not to steal. Lord, You have been clear that I should not take things that are not mine. I also ask that You keep me honest in my personal and business dealings.

9. You have commanded that I must not testify falsely against anyone. Lord, You have been clear that I should not lie and bear false witness against others. I ask that You give me a spirit of integrity.

10. You have commanded that I must not covet anything that someone else has. Lord, You have been clear that I should not covet things that other people have. Lord, I ask that You draw me nearer to You so that I keep my focus on You and not on the things of this world.

Lord, thank You for these 10 Commandments, I praise You for guiding my life each day.

In Jesus' name I pray,
Amen

Joshua 3:16 NLT

The water above that point began backing up a great distance away at a town called Adam, which is near Zarethan. And the water below that point flowed on to the Dead Sea until the riverbed was dry. Then all the people crossed over near the town of Jericho.

Joshua 3:16 NLT

3:16 Biblical Context

Timeline of Joshua 1:1-9, 3:1-17, 4:1-21

- **Joshua 1:1-9** – After Moses' death God appointed Joshua to lead the people and He charged Joshua with a command to be strong and courageous and that the Lord would be with him wherever he went.
- **Joshua 3:1-6** – The people follow Joshua's commands and follow the Ark of the Covenant to the Jordan River, where they purified themselves for the next day's journey across it. The next morning Joshua told the priests to lift the Ark and move out. The Israelites followed.
- **Joshua 3:7** – God told Joshua that He was going to make Joshua a great leader in the eyes of the Israelites.
- **Joshua 3:8-17** – Following God's guidance, Joshua had the Levites carrying the Ark lead the people across the Jordan on dry land.
- **Joshua 4: 1-13** – God commands that they pick 12 stones to commemorate what God had done.
- **Joshua 4:14-21** – The Lord used this event to make Joshua a great leader just as He said He would. Joshua was as revered as his predecessor Moses had been. Joshua made a memorial out of the 12 stones taken from the Jordan River, just east of Jericho, where the Israelites camped.

EXPLORING Joshua 3:16

The phrase, "Where God guides, God provides" is often quoted and could easily have been Joshua's motto. God guided Joshua to be the Israelite leader after Moses' death, and guided Joshua to take the Israelites to the banks of the Jordan, where Joshua told the Israelites, "Today you will know that the living God is among you." (Joshua 3:10a)

Joshua 3:16 finds Joshua just prior to the miracle that is about to take place, standing close enough to see the Jordan River overflowing its banks. Joshua knows that he is at the end of his ability to make things happen. To get through this, Joshua and the Israelites will need to rely on God to provide a way for them. And what a way God provides!

As they crossed that dry riverbed, God had Joshua choose 12 men, one from each tribe, and instructed each of them to choose a stone from the center of the riverbed. The 12 stones were used to build a memorial in remembrance of what God had done. It's amazing the things that God will do in your life when you choose to let God guide your steps.

John 3:16 Correlation: God's provision in removing obstacles and guiding His people on a path to salvation is the underlying theme in this correlation. In Joshua 3:16, God guides His people to the Jordan River, and miraculously provides a way across it. This act of deliverance marks the turning point, where God provides a way for His people to step into a new life He has prepared for them.

Similarly, in John 3:16, God provides a way to eternal life through His Son, Jesus. Just as He removed the physical barrier of the Jordan, allowing His people to enter their promised land, God removes the barrier of sin through Christ's sacrifice, granting us access to a new and eternal life. Both passages reveal God's love and power to overcome obstacles, demonstrating His desire for His people to experience His promises fully, whether in the physical land of Canaan or the spiritual promise of eternal life in Christ.

Something to Think About:

Joshua 3:16 shows how God guided His people through the seemingly impassable obstacle of the Jordan River then provided a way for them to walk across it on dry ground.

3:16 Reflect & Connect

Think about the times when God guided and provided for you. Use the 12 stones to write things God has done for you and make this a place of remembrance in your life. Write something in each of the 12 stones.

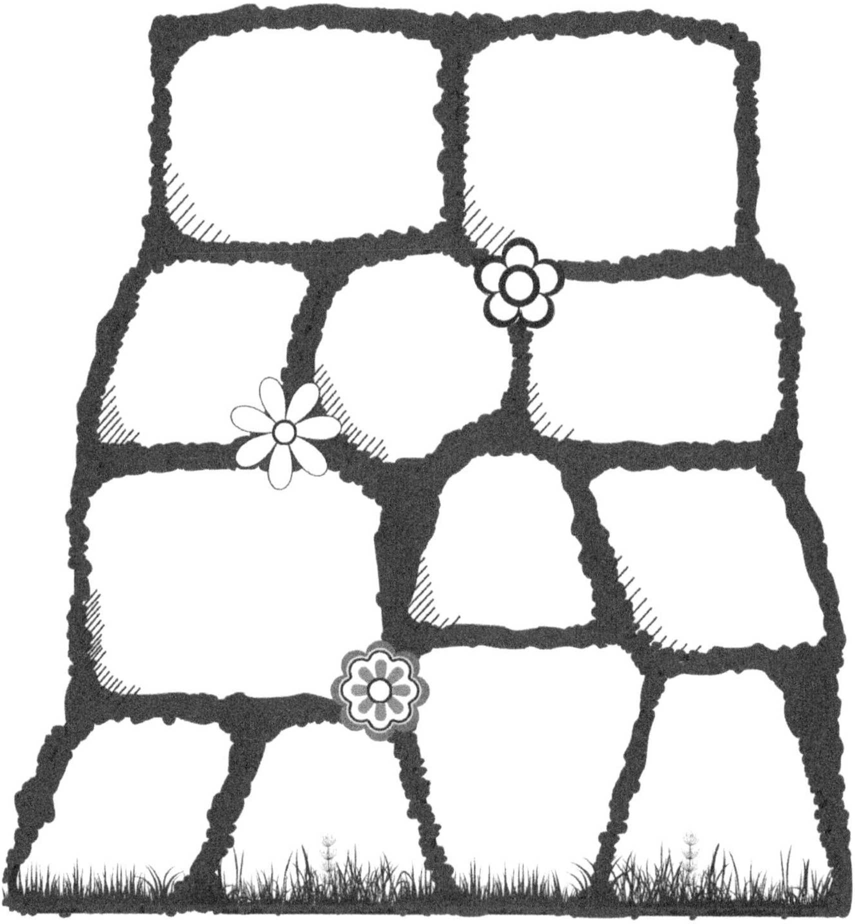

Closing 3:16 Prayer

Heavenly Father,

As I look at the things I have written on these 12 stones, I am in awe of all that You have given me. Lord, I ask forgiveness for not always remembering that You are the giver of all that is good in my life. Your provision in all areas of my life is a blessing and I want to remain grateful.

In Jesus' name I pray,
Amen

Let all that I am
praise the Lord;
may I never forget
the good things
He does for me.

Psalm 103:2 NLT

Judges 3:16 NLT

So Ehud made a double-edged dagger that was about a foot long, and he strapped it to his right thigh, keeping it hidden under his clothing.

Judges 3:16 NLT

3:16 Biblical Context

Timeline of Judges 3:1-4:1

- ✧ **Judges 3:1-6** – Those living in the promised land were generations removed from Moses and Joshua. The Israelites did not seek the Lord, began to intermarry with those nations left in Canaan, and started serving false gods.
- ✧ **Judges 3: 7-11** – The time of the Judges has begun. The Israelites continued to do evil in the sight of the Lord, God got angry and allowed one of the Canaanite nations to conquer them to teach the Israelites a lesson. The Israelites repented. God heard their cry and peace was restored for a generation.
- ✧ **Judges 3:12-15** – Ehud was raised up to save the wayward Israelites while delivering their tribute money to the Moabite King.
- ✧ **Judges 3:16-29** – Ehud uses the knife he crafted and strapped to his thigh to kill the King and restore victory over Moab. Peace remained in the land for 80 years.
- ✧ **Judges 3:31** – Upon Ehud's death, once again, the Israelites did evil in the sight of the Lord.

Exploring Judges 3:16

This 3:16 gives us a picture of a man crafting a double-edged dagger which he straps to his thigh and hides under his clothes. However, the context surrounding the verse is a moment in the history of the Judges, that Israel repeats over and over again.

Joshua is long buried and a new generation of Israelites has come to power. Instead of doing what the Lord had taught them, they turned away from God and intermarried with the nations around them and began to worship false gods. God gets angry and allows one of those nations to conquer the Israelites. The Israelites cry out to God in repentance and from amongst them God raises a Judge to save them from their captivity, restoring peace and putting them back in power.

Judges 3:16 brings us to the time of the 2nd judge, Ehud, who was needed because this generation of Israelites once again went back to worshiping other gods and began serving Baal. Ehud was sent to the Israelites who had lost control of Jericho. Ehud took the dagger we read about in this 3:16 and killed the Moabite King, then led the Israelite army to a sound victory over Moab. His bravery allowed peace for 80 years.

Knowing what we know now, we want to warn the Israelites to repent and follow the one true God. Yet every generation for hundreds of years were pulled away by the temptations of the world around them. This is a lesson we as followers of Christ should take to heart. Let us learn from the Israelites' mistakes, no god is greater than our God!

John 3:16 Correlation: God uses the unexpected to deliver His people and bring about redemption. In Judges 3:16, Ehud, an unlikely hero, is chosen by God to deliver Israel from oppression under the Moabites. Through this unexpected leader, God rescues His people, showing that His ways of deliverance are often surprising and unconventional.

In John 3:16, God again uses the unexpected to bring about salvation—sending His own Son, born in a manager, to offer eternal life through His sacrificial death on the cross. Just as Ehud's deliverance was unexpected but effective, Jesus' crucifixion was, to many, an unforeseen path to salvation. Both passages reveal God's willingness to work through surprising ways to rescue and redeem His people.

3:16 Reflect & Connect

Take a minute and think of the ways you continually fail God. It might be a sin that continues to entangle you, or something that God has asked you to do and you are resistant to doing. Rather than writing the way you have failed God, use these lines to commit to ways that you can be faithful in serving God. Years from now you can find this passage and be able to see that when God gives you strength to do something, you will surely succeed.

Commit everything you do to the Lord. Trust Him and He will help you.

Psalm 37:5 NLT

Closing 3:16 Prayer

Heavenly Father,

Your word is a powerful reminder of how Your people continue to fall away from You. I repent for the ways I have continued to fail You in my life. I pray for these areas that continually trip me up ________________ and I commit myself to You in these ways ________________.

In Jesus' name I pray,

Amen

Ruth 3:16 NIV

When Ruth came to her mother-in-law, Naomi asked, "How did it go, my daughter?" Ruth told Naomi everything Boaz had done for her,

Ruth 3:16 NIV

3:16 Biblical Context

Timeline of Ruth 3:1-4:13

- **Ruth 3:1-5** – Naomi came up with a plan to ensure that her daughter-in-law was provided for and sent Ruth to Boaz.
- **Ruth 3:6-17** – Boaz was a good man and provided for the immediate hunger needs of Ruth, and began a plan to ensure that she would be taken care of.
- **Ruth 4:1-12** – Boaz went through all the proper channels to secure a place for Ruth.
- **Ruth 4:13** – Ruth and Boaz got married and had a son.

"But Ruth replied, 'Don't urge me to leave you or to turn back from you. Where you go I will go, and where you stay I will stay. Your people will be my people and your God my God. Where you die I will die, and there I will be buried. May the Lord deal with me, be it ever so severely, if even death separates you and me.'" Ruth 1:16-17 NIV

EXPLORING Ruth 3:16

The book of Ruth has three main people:

Naomi – The wife of Elimelek and mother of Mahlon and Kilion. Naomi experienced the loss of her husband and both sons, at a time in history when a woman without a man to provide for her would have been unprotected. Naomi planned to go back to her people to find her closest living male relative to be her guardian-redeemer. Prepared to say goodbye to her 2 daughter-in-laws, Naomi planned to send them back to their respective families so they would be protected.

Ruth – With her husband Mahlon deceased, Ruth resisted her mother-in-law's attempt to send her back to her family, determined to stay with Naomi. Ruth's commitment to remain with her mother-in-law to the end is expressed beautifully in Ruth 1:16-17. So Naomi returned to Bethlehem with Ruth by her side.

Boaz – A kind farmer and relative of Naomi. Boaz showed compassion to Ruth who was a foreigner from the despised land of Moab. In the end Boaz took Ruth as his wife and they had a son, Obed, who became the father of Jesse, who became the father of King David.

REDEEMER

This book of the Bible is a fascinating read of those 3 lives intertwined for the Glory of God. This is also a powerful story that redefined what a family looks like. These 3 were not closely connected yet they forged the bonds of family, each stepping outside of what was expected of them. Ultimately, God used this to bring about the lineage of Jesus.

God can work in your life in unexpected ways. Just as God used a widow's strong mind to set in motion a plan that He designed, a woman from a foreign land to carry forth the line of Jesus, and the cleverness and honesty of a farmer to bring this story to completeness, God can use you to bring together things for His good.

John 3:16 Correlation: Ruth 3:16 unveils more of God's plan of redemption and provision as Ruth returns to her mother-in-law, Naomi, after meeting Boaz on the threshing floor. Boaz, acting with kindness and integrity, has taken steps to protect and provide for Ruth, offering her hope for a secure future. This moment foreshadows Boaz's role as a redeemer who will ultimately restore Ruth and Naomi's family line.

Similarly, in John 3:16, God provides the ultimate Redeemer through His Son, Jesus, to offer eternal security and salvation to all who believe. Just as Boaz extends grace and provision to Ruth, Jesus extends God's love to the world, offering a path to redemption and an everlasting relationship with God. Both passages emphasize God's heart to redeem and restore, showing that His love leads to lasting security and hope.

Something to Think About:

Ruth's vow to Naomi

"...Where you go I will go,
and where you stay I will stay.
Your people will be my people and
your God my God..."

Led Ruth to her Redeemer

*How might our own loyalty and
faith open doors to blessings
we can't even imagine?*

3:16 Reflect & Connect

Ruth 3:16 is the beginning of a love story. On the lines below, write about the prompt that best fits your life:

- ♥ **Write your love story.**
- ♥ **Look to someone in your life who has the kind of relationship you would like to have one day. Write things about this couple that inspire you. Then pray that God will give you patience to wait on the person He has for you.**

Closing 3:16 Prayer

Heavenly Father,

I come to You today, asking that You chip away at the parts of me that do not please you. Make me like Naomi who thought of others first and found ways to connect them. Make me like Ruth who was faithful in all things, even when it was hard. Make me like Boaz who was good and righteous and looked out for others.

In Jesus' name I pray,
Amen

1 Samuel 3:16 ESV

But Eli called Samuel and said, "Samuel, my son." and he said "Here I am."

1 Samuel 3:16 ESV

3:16 Biblical Context

Timeline of 1 Samuel 1:21-3:21

- **1 Samuel 1:21-2:11** – Hannah brings Samuel to serve the Lord, to fulfill her vow to the Lord.
- **1 Samuel 2:12-17** – Eli's sons treat the offerings of the Lord with contempt.
- **1 Samuel 2:18-21** – Samuel grew up serving the Lord by assisting Eli the priest.
- **1 Samuel 2:22-36** – Samuel was audibly called by God on 3 different occasions however Samuel had never received a call from God so he assumed the voice was that of the priest Eli. On the third time Samuel went to Eli, the priest realized it was the Lord calling Samuel and told the boy to respond to the Lord when he heard the call again. God told Samuel that He was going to hold Israel, Eli, and his sons accountable.
- **1 Samuel 3:1-18** – God wants Samuel to tell Eli what the Lord had said to him. God reveals His plan to judge Eli's household. Though afraid, Samuel faithfully conveys God's message to Eli.
- **1 Samuel 3:19-21** – God continued to speak to Samuel and he became recognized as a reliable prophet.

Here I am Lord

EXPLORING 1 Samuel 3:16

Imagine taking a nap and being awakened by your name being called. Your response would probably be the same as Samuel's, going to Eli to see what he wanted. Like Samuel, it would probably take you several times to realize that it was God Himself calling you. After all, why would God be calling your name? That's exactly how it happened with Samuel in the verses leading up to this 3:16.

Samuel wakes to the sound of his name and mistakenly thinks it is Eli. When Eli denies calling him, Samuel heads back to bed. When this happens the 3rd time, Eli realizes God is calling Samuel and tells Samuel, if you hear it again, say, 'speak Lord, your servant is listening.' Fortunately, God is patient, and when He called Samuel again, this time the boy knew what to do.

Can you imagine how hard it would have been for young Samuel to tell Eli that God was going to carry out His punishment of Eli and his sons? In the morning, Eli demanded to know exactly what the Lord told Samuel, and although he was nervous, Samuel shared what God had told him, and Eli accepted Samuel's words as God's will.

Something to Think About

Since Adam & Eve, God has revealed Himself to very few people, yet He revealed Himself to Samuel at Shiloh.

Do you think God misses being able to physically walk and talk with us?

3:16 Reflect & Connect

As we saw with Samuel, God speaks to us, though rarely the way He did in the story above.

✦ Write verses that God has used to speak to you. Look through your Bible at verses you have highlighted or notes you have written in the margin.

✦ Write about a time God has spoken to you through someone else's words. (Conversations, sermons & Bible studies etc.)

✦ How did you know it was God speaking to you?

✦ If you can't think of anything, go ask a Christian friend or family member about times in their life God has spoken to them. Listen to the ways that they knew it was God speaking and write them here.

GOD

hears the Cries

of a woman's

Heart

and answers in ways

GREATER

than we can

Imagine

Closing 3:16 Prayer

Heavenly Father,

Please help me to be attentive when You are speaking to me. Make me aware of the times You would like me to speak Your truth into someone's life. Give me the courage to speak Your words, even when it's hard. Lord, I will be faithful to go and speak to ____________ as You give me the opportunity.

In Jesus' name I pray,

Amen

Make me to know Your ways, O Lord; teach me Your paths. Lead me in Your truth and teach me, for You are the God of my salvation; for You I wait all the day long.

Psalm 25:4-5 ESV

2 Samuel 3:16 NLT

Palti followed along behind her as far as Bahurim, weeping as he went. Then Abner told him, "Go back home!" So Palti returned.

2 Samuel 3:16 NLT

3:16 Biblical Context

Timeline of 2 Samuel 3:1-16

- **2 Samuel 3:1** – This chapter starts by explaining the war raging between David and the house of Saul.
- **2 Samuel 3:6-13** – After an insult from Saul's son, Abner changed his loyalty from Saul's house to David.
- **2 Samuel 3:14-16** – David, in a deeply political move, wanted his first wife Michal back, so she was taken from her husband Palti and returned back to David.

Exploring 2 Samuel 3:16

This verse can be a little difficult to decipher without a bit of background. The "she" in this verse is Michal, the younger daughter of King Saul. We first meet Michal in 1 Samuel when she falls in love with David. King Saul eventually gave Michal to David as his wife. Michal's love for her husband made Saul even more jealous of David, and Saul finally decided to just kill him. Michal helped David escape by deceiving her father. This was the last time Michal and David saw each other until Saul is dead and David demands her return.

You would think that this would bring about a happy ending to their love story, but during David's exile and subsequent rise to power Saul had given Michal to Palti in marriage and Palti loved Michal deeply. When David sent Abner to bring Michal back to his house. Palti was noticeably upset and had followed Michal's carriage, weeping until he was told by Abner to "go back."

John 3:16 Correlation: Doesn't your heart just break for Michal? To experience the love of two men, and be forced to sacrifice that love twice to circumstances beyond your control. 2 Samuel 3:16 shows us a painful scene of separation, reflecting the personal sacrifices and deep costs involved in the unfolding of God's plans for Israel's future, particularly as David moves closer to fulfilling his role as King.

In John 3:16, God's plan for redemption also involves a profound sacrifice, this time, His own son, given out of love to provide eternal life for humanity. Just as Michal's separation from Palti led to the establishment of Israel's kingdom, Jesus' sacrificial death led to the establishment of God's eternal kingdom, available to all who believe.

Something to Think About

Through every situation in our lives, both good and bad, God gives us opportunities to grow. The choice of how you grow, is up to you.

3:16 Reflect & Connect

The deep care that we see from Palti, grieving for his wife, is very sweet, yet it shows how little some women were considered in Biblical times. Sadly, this is still true for women and girls in a few areas of the world. Think about children, young people, and adults in our world that are marginalized or living in unsafe places. Now think of girls or young women in your own life and the pressures and challenges they face. If you feel able to do this, write or text something to these young ladies. Let them know that you value them and share with them how important they are in your life.

I prayed for:____

____

I wrote/texted:______________________________________

____

I spoke directly to:___________________________________

____

Closing 3:16 Prayer

Heavenly Father,

There are children, young people, and adults around this globe who are living in places that are not safe. Lord, I know that You care for every last one of them. Lord, I know that there will always be wars and threats of war in our world, I pray that You will be with those who are in war torn areas. I also lift up the children and adults around our world who have been enslaved in human trafficking. Please hold them close, Lord, and I ask that You provide a way out for them.

In Jesus' name I pray,

Amen

"The name of the Lord is a strong fortress; the Godly run to Him and are safe."

Proverbs 18:10 NLT

1 Kings 3:16 NLT

Some time later two prostitutes came to the king to have an argument settled.

1 Kings 3:16 NLT

3:16 Biblical Context

Timeline of 1 Kings 3:3-27

- ✧ **1 Kings 3:3-15** – Solomon has become King of Israel and speaks with God, asking for wisdom. God is pleased with Solomon and gives him wisdom, while also blessing him with wealth and a long life.
- ✧ **1 Kings 3:16-27** – Solomon shows wisdom with the case of 2 mothers.
- ✧ **1 Kings 3:28** – Everyone heard about Solomon's wise decision and recognized that he had been given wisdom by God.

Exploring 1 Kings 3:16

This one verse may not seem familiar, however, you may know this story...

Some time after Solomon became the King of Israel, two women came before him to have an argument settled. Both women had babies around the same time and one of the infant's died during the night. The mother of the baby who had died took her lifeless child and placed it with the other mother and took the living child back to her own room. After telling their story to the King, the women bickered over who was the rightful mother. King Solomon ordered a sword to be brought and he told them that he would cut the child in half and give one half to each woman.

The actual mother cried out NO, give the baby to the other woman, don't kill him. She was willing to give him up to the other woman so that he would live. King Solomon immediately recognized that the woman who chose to save the child's life was the true mother.

3:16 Reflect & Connect

There is so much going on in this biblical story, if you are not familiar with it you may want to read back through the story. Take note of the fact that the wisest king to ever rule the Israelites chose to settle an argument between 2 prostitutes. In Jewish society, Solomon sat at the very top, while the 2 women in this story sat very near the bottom. Yet King Solomon treated them as fairly as he would anyone who came before him, and rendered his judgment in such a wise way that the rightful mother got to walk away with her son in her arms.

Wisdom is something that we should all want to have. In theory, we will gain wisdom as we age, but it doesn't hurt to have a reminder. Write out a "Life Verse for Wisdom". Find a verse that inspires you to seek wisdom, such as Psalm 90:12 or James 1:5, and write it out in the area provided below. Surround it with doodles, decorative borders, or calligraphy to make it stand out as a personal reminder.

Life Verse for Wisdom

Think of the wisdom the King used in this challenging situation. Now jot down some times where you have been asked to give someone advice, or times when you have given unsolicited advice. In those situations, have you stopped to ask God for guidance first? If not, pray now for wisdom when you have to give advice, and ask God to remind you to seek Him first.

Something to Think About

Solomon's most famous judgment dealt with women in need, who couldn't solve their problem.

Who do you turn to for wisdom when you need a solution?

FOR THE LORD GRANTS WISDOM!

FROM HIS MOUTH COME KNOWLEDGE AND UNDERSTANDING. PROVERBS 2:6

Closing 3:16 Prayer

Heavenly Father,

I come to You today asking for wisdom in ____________ area of my life. God I am prone to run ahead of You and I ask forgiveness for areas of my life that I fail to seek You first. God I praise You for the wisdom of Solomon and make a commitment to seek You more closely in my day to day life.

In Jesus' name I pray,

Amen

2 Kings 3:16 NLT

and he said, "This is what the Lord says: This dry valley will be filled with pools of water!

2 Kings 3:16 NLT

3:16 Biblical Context

Timeline of 2 Kings 3:4-20

- ✧ **2 Kings 3:4-7** – Two Kings joined forces against the Moab King after he refused to pay his tribute.
- ✧ **2 Kings 3:8-9** – The 2 King's armies were joined by a 3rd King's army and marched through the wilderness of Edom for 7 days on their way to battle Moab. There was no water when they got there, and the men began to fear for their lives.
- ✧ **2 Kings 3:10-15a** – The 3 Kings conferred and sought the council of Elisha who was known to be a man who studied under the prophet Elijah.
- ✧ **2 Kings 3:15b-20** – Elisha received word from the Lord that there would be enough water for the men and animals, and also that the Israelite armies would be successful at conquering the Moab army.

Exploring 2 Kings 3:16

This 3:16 is a conversation between Elisha and the 2 Israelite King's along with Edom's King. Elisha is sharing with the Kings that God will deliver Moab into their hands. The Lord is going to fill the valley with pools of water for their cattle and armies to drink even though there wouldn't be any wind or rain. These things happened the next morning and it set the battle in motion. The Moabites saw the water and when the sun shone on the water, it looked red. This caused the Moabite army to think it was the blood of the 3 armies and they rushed in. When they entered Israel's camp, the Israelites rose up and attacked and conquered the Moabites.

3:16 Reflect & Connect

This 3:16 is an example of how one verse can lead us into a riveting account of God's power. Think of a time when God led you to do something, and how that helped you to step out in faith and do something you didn't think you were capable of doing. Write that situation here so you can always look back and see how useful you are in the Kingdom of God .

Something to Think About:

The Kings of the 3 armies prepared their troops for battle, but were unprepared for the lack of water when they got close to Moab. Their need for water was not a problem they could solve. The prophet Elisha went with the armies, not expecting to be asked for a word from the Lord. Yet he was faithful, and gave them the words from the Lord that miraculously solved their need for water, and delivered Moab into their hands.

When the unexpected happens what do you do?

Closing 3:16 Prayer

Heavenly Father,

Reading this passage has reminded me of the times You have used me to benefit Your kingdom. God, I ask that You give me more opportunities to be a blessing. I pray that You allow me to use the following talents that You have given me, ________________________________ to serve Your Kingdom this week.

In Jesus' name I pray,
Amen

1 Chronicles 3:16 NASB

The sons of Jehoiakim were his son Jehoiachin and his son Zedekiah.

1 Chronicles 3:16 NASB

3:16 Biblical Context

Timeline of 1 Chronicles 3: 10-16

✧ **1 Chronicles 3:10-16** – Part of the listing of the line of David, beginning with David's son Solomon and leading to Jehoiakim.

Exploring 1 Chronicles 3:16

At first, this verse may not capture your attention. Three names of men in the Bible whom you may not know. However, Chapter 3 is the part of the Genealogy of Judah that centers around the family line of David. This is important because back in 2 Samuel 7, God promised David that the Messiah would come from David's lineage. 1 Chronicles 1-3, is the beginning of that proof, as it establishes David's lineage from Judah, son of Jacob, son of Isaac, son of Abraham. Then proceeds to trace David's line through Solomon and continues on down David's line.

This just goes to show you that the long genealogies in the scripture that may seem tedious and dry, are there for a very good reason. History can serve to remind us that God is faithful and He can use whomever He chooses to bring about His perfect will.

John 3:16 Correlation: Throughout these correlations, we have seen God's plan for our redemption unfolding, and even this seemingly boring verse plays its part. 1 Chronicles 3:16 lists the descendants of Jehoiakim, part of the royal line of David. This lineage is significant because it eventually leads to Jesus, the fulfillment of God's promise to bring salvation through the line of David.

John 3:16 reveals the purpose of this lineage: God sent His Son, Jesus, so that through Him, the world might have eternal life. Together, these verses point to how God carefully prepared and fulfilled His plan for our salvation through the generations.

3:16 Reflect & Connect

1 Chronicles is not just a book full of genealogies, this is where we get a retelling of the death of King Saul and David crowning his son Solomon as King. 1 Chronicles also gives us some new stories about David that can't be found anywhere else in the Bible. If it has been a while since you have read 1 Chronicles, make a commitment to yourself to read some or all of this powerful book of the Bible by the date you have written here.

____

David shares with his son Solomon to,

> "Be strong and courageous, Get to work, Don't be afraid or discouraged, because the Lord God, my God, is with you. He'll neither let you down nor leave you before all the work for the service of the Lord's temple is done."
>
> 1 Chronicles 28:20 NLT

Meditate on this and circle or highlight the words or phrases that are meaningful to you.

This 3:16 gave us the names of 3 family members of David's lineage. Take a few moments to think about the people God has placed in your family. There may be some family members who are unsafe to be around, or those who have hurt you in ways that make forgiveness difficult. Take some time to talk to God about this. Let Him have your hurt, your anger, your fear, and/or your trauma, His shoulders are vast & His arms are waiting to hold you. Take this first step toward healing.

A good rule of thumb to follow when praying for those you consider family: remember family by blood, by adoption, and family that have come into your life through foster care or by choice.

After you pray, consider setting an alarm on your phone for 3:16 p.m. to help you remember to pray for them every day.

SOMETHING TO THINK ABOUT

Israel & Judah had 42 Kings & 1 Queen

Most of whom did evil in the sight of the Lord. Only 7 of those Kings did what was right in the sight of the Lord. 4 more did both good and evil, with 1 unknown. That leaves 30 Kings & 1 Queen who did evil in the sight of the Lord. Only those who obeyed God their whole reign prospered.

What do you think God is trying to tell you?

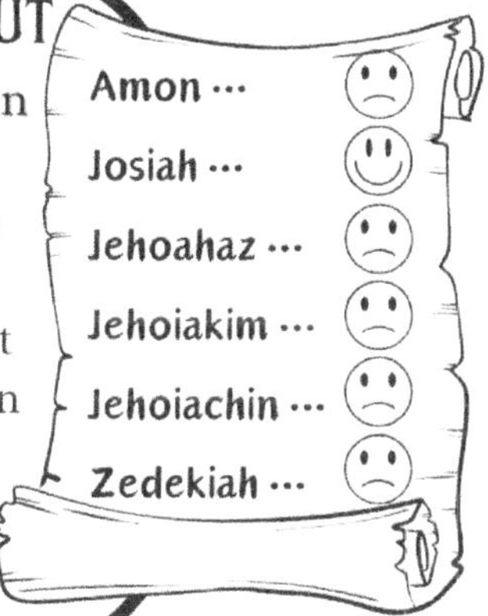

Closing 3:16 PRAYER

David has a powerful song of praise in 1 Chronicles 16:8-36, so part of this closing prayer will be praying these verses back to God. If you are unfamiliar with praying scripture to God, you can do this in a number of ways. You can read the words as they are said or you can modify the directionality by speaking directly to God.

Example:

Splendor and majesty are before Him; strength and joy are in His dwelling place. (direct quote from 1 Chronicles 16:27)

Splendor and majesty are before You Lord, strength and joy are in Your dwelling place. (directed toward God by shifting tense and pronouns)

Heavenly Father,

My whole life should be about praising You. When I rise in the morning, before I go to sleep at night, and all the moments in between are opportunities to give You praise. Psalm 34:1 says, "I will praise the Lord at all times. I will constantly sing His praises." During both the blessings and the trials I will praise You. Through the good and the bad in my life I will praise You.

I praise You now with the words of David from

1 Chronicles 16:23-36 NIV

Sing to the Lord all the earth; proclaim His salvation day after day.
Declare His glory among the nations, His marvelous deeds among all peoples.
For great is the Lord and most worthy of praise; He is to be feared above all gods.
For all the gods of the nations are idols, but the Lord made the heavens.
Splendor and majesty are before Him; strength and joy are in His dwelling place.
Ascribe to the Lord, all You families of nations, ascribe to the Lord glory and strength.
Ascribe to the Lord the glory due His name; bring an offering and come before Him. Worship the Lord in the splendor of His Holiness.
Tremble before Him, all the earth! The world is firmly established; it cannot be moved.
Let the heavens rejoice, let the earth be glad; let them say among the nations, "The Lord reigns!"
Let the sea resound, and all that is in it; let the fields be jubilant, and everything in them!
Let the trees of the forest sing, let them sing for joy before the Lord, for He comes to judge the earth.
Give thanks to the Lord, for He is good; His love endures forever.
Cry out, "Save us, God our Savior; gather us and deliver us from the nations, that we may give thanks to Your holy name, and glory in Your praise."
Praise be to the Lord, the God of Israel, from everlasting to everlasting.
In Jesus' name I pray,

Amen

Be
Strong
&
Courageous
1 Chronicles 28:20

2 Chronicles 3:16 NLT

He made a network of interwoven chains and used them to decorate the tops of the pillars. He also made 100 decorative pomegranates and attached them to the chains.

2 Chronicles 3:16 NLT

3:16 Biblical Context

Timeline of 2 Chronicles 3:1-17

- **2 Chronicles 3:1-2** – Description of when and where the Temple was built.
- **2 Chronicles 3:3-7** – Description of building the main part of the Temple.
- **2 Chronicles 3:8-14** – Description of building the Most Holy Place.
- **2 Chronicles 3:15-17** – Description of building the front of the Temple.

For further reading about the building of the Temple of the Lord, see 1 Kings 6

Exploring 2 Chronicles 3:16

When reading the Chronicles, it is important to remember that 1 & 2 Chronicles were originally written as one book and they were split into 2 books due to scroll length.

As we know from 1 Kings 6, Solomon was tasked with building the Temple of the Lord. The 2 Chronicles version focuses on the Temple itself, giving us a clear picture of what the building looked like.

Depending on which version of the Bible you read, some of the terminology for the dimensions of the temple are not familiar to modern day readers.

If you struggle to understand the measurements and adornments listed in this passage, find a version that is easier to comprehend.

2 Chronicles 3:16 gives us a look at one of the adornments - 100 decorative pomegranates. This fruit is as unique as its name, shaped somewhere between an oval and a hexagon with a small node at the top. The bold red color sets it apart from other fruits, making this an ideal adornment to cascade down the entrance pillars of the temple. The author of 2 Chronicles is unknown yet his inclusion of the beautiful adornment of the temple in his description of how it was built, gives us a picture of the beauty that could not be ignored in the overall description of the Temple.

John 3:16 Correlation: Once again we see God's desire to dwell with His people, and provide a way for them to come to Him. 2 Chronicles 3:16 describes just one small part of the intricate design that Solomon put into the Temple he built for God to dwell in so He could have a more personal relationship with His people through their worship and sacrifice.

In John 3:16, God's plan comes to fruition through our worship because of Jesus's sacrifice on the cross. Now, our bodies have become God's temple, His dwelling place, and we can have a personal relationship with Him.

3:16 Reflect & Connect

In 2 Chronicles 3, we see Solomon building the Temple of the Lord. This 3:16 speaks about decorations that would adorn the entrance of the Temple. Since our bodies are God's Temple now, let's take a moment to consider how we compare to the Temple that Solomon built.

Reading the ornate beauty used to adorn the interior of the Temple, it is clear that God is much more interested in how beautiful we are on the inside. With this in mind, we should live our lives in a manner pleasing to God.

On the lines below, list some things that you choose to do to honor God.

Knowing that your body is His Temple, write some ways that you care or will care for your spiritual and physical well-being.

During your closing prayer, ask the Lord to help you do or continue to do the things you wrote above, and also ask Him to help you stop doing things that do not glorify God.

For today's Bible journal, go find a craft/activity that you enjoy and spend some time doing that. If your craft/activity allows you to think such as gardening or completing a puzzle, use that time to pray. When your craft/activity is complete, look at the completed craft and praise God for giving you time to do this and for giving you a creative mind to be able to make something that decorates your space like Solomon decorated the temple of the Lord.

The craft or activity I completed today was:

Closing 3:16 Prayer

Heavenly Father,

Thank You for sending Your Son Jesus to die on the cross so that I might live as Your Temple. Please help me to live my life in a manner that is pleasing to You. Thank you for blessing me with a creative mind and for giving me a bit of time to enjoy a craft today. Lord, I thank You for these times in my life when I can enjoy these activities.

In Jesus' name I pray,

Amen

Nehemiah 3:16 NLT

Next to him was Nehemiah son of Azbuk, the leader of half the district of Beth-zur. He rebuilt the wall from a place across from the tombs of David's family as far as the water reservoir and the House of the Warriors.

Nehemiah 3:16 NLT

3:16 Biblical Context

Timeline of Nehemiah 1:1-3:32 & 6:15

- **Nehemiah 1:1-11** – Nehemiah hears about the damage done to Jerusalem's walls.
- **Nehemiah 2:1-15** – Nehemiah sets out to see the damaged walls of Jerusalem.
- **Nehemiah 2:16-20** – Nehemiah states that God has taken care of him during his inspection of the walls and rallies the people to start rebuilding.
- **Nehemiah 3:1-32** – Multiple accounts of groups of people who helped in the rebuilding of the walls.
- **Nehemiah 6:15**- The wall was finished, taking 52 days to complete.

Exploring Nehemiah 3:16

The book of Nehemiah, is the memoirs of Nehemiah son of Hacaliah. However, for clarity, there is also a second Nehemiah, the son of Azbuk, and he is the Nehemiah who is being talked about in this 3:16.

In the book of Nehemiah, the walls of Jerusalem are being rebuilt. These walls had been destroyed, and its gates burned 150 years prior to Nehemiah. Yet as soon as Nehemiah heard the news he sat down and wept, mourning for days, fasting, and praying, crying out to the God of heaven.

Nehemiah was sent by God to inspect the walls of Jerusalem, rally everyone he could, and get the rebuild started.

Chapter 3 is speaking about the repairs done on the walls and gates surrounding Jerusalem. We see that the city came together to help, each using their own talents to rebuild Jerusalem's walls and gates. Priests and tradespeople worked together to accomplish this task. In Nehemiah 3:12, we see Shallum, leader of half the district of Jerusalem, and his daughters helped with the rebuilding.

The walls of Jerusalem, which had lay in ruins for 150 years, were rebuilt in 52 days, and Nehemiah was made governor of Jerusalem. One grieving heart, sincerely crying out to God can bring His people together to accomplish great things.

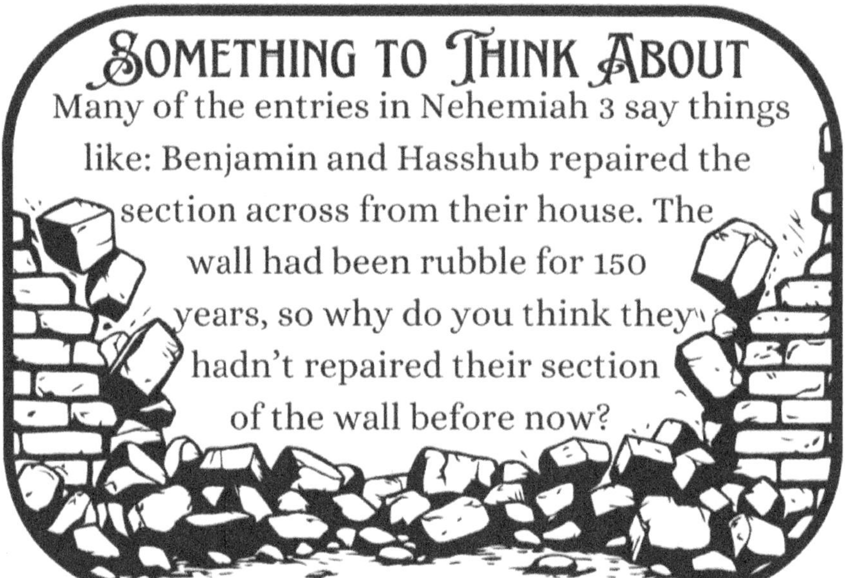

Something to Think About

Many of the entries in Nehemiah 3 say things like: Benjamin and Hasshub repaired the section across from their house. The wall had been rubble for 150 years, so why do you think they hadn't repaired their section of the wall before now?

3:16 Reflect & Connect

Think about ways you can help to support your local church. Use the skills that God has given you to be a blessing to the house of the Lord. If you are skilled in repair/electric skills, ask your church leader if there is something around the church that might need attention. If you are skilled in more creative endeavors, offer to decorate for a holiday or create a mural for the children's ministry.

God has uniquely gifted you and loves when you use those talents to serve Him. On the lines below, write ways that you will commit to support your church with the talents He has given you.

____

____

____

____

____

____

GOD-GiVEN TALENTS

Closing 3:16 PRAYER

Heavenly Father,

You have gifted me with talents that I can use to bless Your church. Thank You for reminding me of the gifts You have given me such as ____________________. I pray that You will allow me an opportunity to use those gifts and I trust that You will lead me to those who can make this project come to life.

In Jesus' name I pray,

Amen

Job 3:16 NLT

Why wasn't I buried like a stillborn child, like a baby who never lives to see the light?

Job 3:16 NLT

3:16 Biblical Context

Timeline of Job 1- 3:26

- **Job 1-2** – God holds Job in high esteem, yet He gives satan permission to test Job's faithfulness. In one day Job lost all of his servants, animals and children, yet Job didn't curse God. So, satan asked God for permission to strike at Job's health, assuming that terrible boils all over his body would surely cause Job to curse God.
- **Job 3: 1-26** – This is Job's first speech to his friends who had come to comfort and console him after his overwhelming loss, the death of his children, and the painful sores afflicting his body.

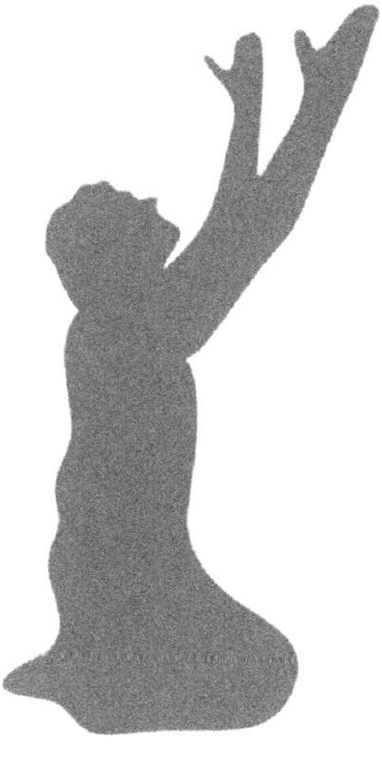

The Lord gave me what I had, and the Lord has taken it away. Praise the name of the Lord!

Job 1:21b NLT

EXPLORING Job 3:16

Reading the book of Job is not easy, as chapter 1 contains a devastating loss for Job. During the next 41 chapters, we see the grief and turmoil Job wrestles with. This blameless man of integrity is being tested. His friends come to sit with Job to offer their support during this time of loss and grief.

In the first chapter of the book of Job, we see his 7 sons and 3 daughters all died when a strong wind came and caused the house they were in to collapse on them.

Then in Chapter 2, Job was tested once again, this time with boils from head to foot, but Job still refused to curse God. Even when Job's wife says to him,

> "Are you still clinging to your integrity? Curse God, and die."
> Job 2:9 CEB

Job reminds her that we must accept the bad as well as the good that comes from the Lord.

This statement that Job's wife makes, has been used to show how she had given up on God and encouraged her husband to do the same. Yet there is no record of God rebuking her. We know she is grieving just as much, if not more than Job. Left, like many women, to grieve silently. Could it be that in her heart wrenching grief at the loss of her 10 children, she was overcome and did not know how else to express it?

As this is the only time we see Job's wife, we will never know. However, it should be noted that when Job's health, wealth and family were restored, Job's wife also reaped the reward for not giving up.

The words found in Job 3:16 can speak directly to women. 15% of women experience a miscarriage, and worldwide there are 2 million stillborn babies each year. The loss of a child growing in your womb can leave a woman feeling guilt and shame and can contribute to mental health issues that last for years. Reading the book of Job can provide understanding of being in the depths of grief and not giving up. Job 42:10-16, the very end of this book, shows that God had not forgotten Job, just as God will not forget you in your time of grief dear sister.

3:16 Reflect & Connect

If you have lost a child, allow yourself to grieve that loss. Talk with God about the pain you feel. If you have not experienced this type of devastating loss, pray for women throughout the world who have lost a child. As you move forward, ask God how you can minister to someone who has lost a child.

When you are done praying, write down something you are going to do this week to help yourself heal, or help someone heal from the loss of a child.

____

____

____

Closing 3:16 Prayer

Heavenly Father,

I don't even know where to begin to grieve the loss of my child. I have wept and my heart aches each time I think of that precious life. Lord help me to begin to come to You with that grief and pain. Help me to know how to move forward in that grief, trusting that You hold my child safe in Your arms. God, I lift up others who have lost children and I ask that You give me a chance to be a blessing to a woman this week who is in need of a friend.

In Jesus' name I pray,

Amen

Proverbs 3:16 NLT

She offers you long life in her right hand, and riches and honor in her left.

Proverbs 3:16 NLT

3:16 Biblical Context

Timeline of Proverbs 1:1- 3:23

- ✧ **Proverbs 1:1-7** – Solomon instructs that the Proverbs are to teach wisdom, discipline, and moral guidance, rooted in reverence for God.
- ✧ **Proverbs 1:8-33** – Emphasizes rejecting evil & embracing wisdom.
- ✧ **Proverbs 2:1-22** – The benefits of allowing God's wisdom into your life.
- ✧ **Proverbs 3:1-23** – Encouraging words on the many benefits of wisdom: it can bring joy, discipline, understanding, and be a guide in your life. It is also a reminder that the wisdom we seek should come directly from the Lord.

Exploring Proverbs 3:16

Proverbs 3:16 seems to be speaking about a woman who is offering you long life, riches and honor. However, if we look at the verse before it, we see that the "she" is wisdom. Verse 15 says, "Wisdom is more precious than rubies; nothing you desire can compare with her". This is why it is so important to read Bible verses in context with the verses and chapters around them.

It can also be helpful to dig a little deeper and read Bible commentaries that offer insight about the verse/passage you are reading. For example: The Hebrew word for wisdom is Chokmah which is grammatically feminine. This explains why Wisdom is referred to as a woman.

If we only read verse 16, we might believe these 2 things.

1. This verse is saying that God is a woman.
2. This verse is saying that you will have a long life, riches and honor.

When we dig into the scripture a bit more, we see that neither of those things are what the scripture is saying, instead we find that wisdom is what we should be seeking, and that wisdom comes directly from our Heavenly Father.

3:16 Reflect & Connect

In our society today, personal choice is the cornerstone of individual freedom and identity. This reflects a shift toward empowering people to make decisions that align with their own unique values & preferences. However, the core tenets of the book of Proverbs are rooted in a reverence for God as the foundation of true knowledge. Proverbs teaches us that rather than our own preferences, we should be looking to God for wisdom.

Wisdom is important for all women, and it's extremely important to pass that wisdom down to the next generation. Today, write a bit of wisdom that your mother/grandmother or a woman of influence in your life shared with you. Then record how that bit of wisdom has served you in your lifetime? Finally, consider who you should pass this wisdom on to, and write their name(s) at the bottom.

Joyful is the person who finds wisdom,
the one who gains understanding.
For wisdom is more profitable than silver,
and her wages are better than gold.

Proverbs 3:13-14 NLT

Closing 3:16 Prayer

Heavenly Father,

I need Your wisdom each day. I am prone to seeking my own way of doing things and it often causes me to miss what You have for me. Lord keep my mind focused on You and remind me of Proverbs 3 when I try to find solutions within myself. God I praise You for the wise women in my life who have shared Your wisdom with me. Help me to be a wise woman, and to seek You continually, as I pass on my wisdom to the next generation.

In Jesus' name I pray,

Amen

Ecclesiastes 3:16 NLT

NLT – I also noticed that under the sun there is evil in the courtroom. Yes, even the courts of law are corrupt!

TLB – Moreover, I notice that throughout the earth justice is giving way to crime, and even the police courts are corrupt.

CEB – I saw something else under the sun: in the place of justice, there was wickedness; and in the place of what was right, there was wickedness again!

KJV – And moreover I saw under the sun the place of judgment, that wickedness was there; and the place of righteousness, that iniquity was there.

NLV – Also I have seen under the sun that in the place of what is right and fair there is sin. And in the place of what is right and good there is wrong-doing.

Message – I took another good look at what's going on: The very place of judgment—corrupt! The place of righteousness—corrupt!

3:16 Biblical Context

Timeline of Ecclesiastes 3:16-4:3

- **Ecclesiastes 3:16** – Solomon is pondering how wickedness has crept into the justice system.
- **Ecclesiastes 3:17** – Solomon acknowledges to himself that good or bad, God will judge everyone.
- **Ecclesiastes 3:18-22** – Solomon determines that everything is meaningless and both humans and animals all start from dust and return to dust.
- **Ecclesiastes 4:1-3** – Solomon also realized that tears and oppression await all, and it would have been better to have never existed, than witness the corruption found on earth.

EXPLORING Ecclesiastes 3:16

Not every passage of God's word is full of lighthearted topics, however, they are all useful in instructing us on how to live our lives. This 3:16 could apply to what is happening in our world today, as it looks at the court system and the corruption that can be found there. Even in this our hope comes from God, because whether justice is served in this life or not, God's justice will be served in the next, as verse 17 reminds us that, "...in due season God will judge everyone, both good and bad, for all their deeds."

This passage of the Bible can easily be summed up as a reminder to be accountable to God, for judgment comes to all. We can look at this as a stern reminder that God is watching all that we do and sees all of our iniquity. Or it can be a place of comfort when corruption and wickedness befall us, we will not be overlooked by our righteous Judge.

3:16 Reflect & Connect

There is value in seeking out scripture in multiple versions. While you probably have a Bible that you are comfortable reading, sometimes there are versions or translations that give you a clearer understanding of what the scripture is saying.

- ✦ Look at all of the different translations of Ecclesiastes 3:16 at the beginning of this chapter.
- ✦ Circle which of these translations is the most relatable to you, and underline the words that stood out to you today.
- ✦ Now look at the version you chose. What was it about the way those words were laid out that caused it to connect with you?

- ✦ If this is not a version of the Bible that you currently own, open an app so you can check it out, you might find that God's word becomes more alive to you as you read it.

Closing 3:16 Prayer

Heavenly Father,

I come to You right now, asking that You move in a mighty way in the court system. Lord, I ask that You work in the lives of the Judges and lawyers who work in the legal system. God I ask that those who do not know You will come to know You and begin to seek You as they consider cases. Lord, I pray specifically for those who work in the legal system in my state.

In Jesus' name I pray,

Amen

Isaiah 3:16 NLT

The Lord says, "Beautiful Zion is haughty: craning her elegant neck, flirting with her eyes, walking with dainty steps, tinkling her ankle bracelets.

Isaiah 3:16 NLT

3:16 Biblical Context

Timeline of Isaiah 2-4

- **Isaiah 2:1-4** – Isaiah is describing what Zion will be- the glory awaiting them in the future.
- **Isaiah 2:5-22** – Isaiah encourages the descendants of Jacob to walk in the Lord's light, and gives a warning of judgment to come.
- **Isaiah 3:1-15** – Isaiah describes the judgment that will fall on the wicked of Judah, while the godly will be well.
- **Isaiah 3:16-26** – A stern warning for those daughters of Zion who have let wealth and vanity corrupt them. Isaiah writes of the doom and shame that are awaiting them.
- **Isaiah 4:1-6** – The glorious future that awaits Zion for those who have remained faithful to the Lord.

Exploring Isaiah 3:16

This 3:16 is the beginning of a passage, Isaiah 3:16-26, in which the description of "beautiful Zion" and its women is not strictly metaphorical, but rather a poetic and prophetic representation of Jerusalem's arrogance, moral decay, and pending judgment.

God often does this, uses something that is happening to draw our awareness to a spiritual need. The women of Jerusalem were full of themselves and had an obsession with beauty. They were flirtatious and attention seeking. These women are examples of the city's vanity, spiritual decline and misplaced priorities. The stripping away of these adornments, and the resulting shame, reflect the judgment that Jerusalem will face for its pride and disobedience.

Criticizing the way that someone behaves is one thing, however Isaiah's words go deeper than their outward appearance, this is a reprimand of their inward thought process. This 3:16 shows us how these women display themselves as flirtatious and attention seeking and reminds us to examine our own inward thoughts.

The literal translation of this verse is "women who think highly of themselves." This is not only a metaphor for the city of Zion, this is speaking to women as well.

3:16 Reflect & Connect

Ladies, we can become full of ourselves, and begin acting in ways unbecoming to God. On the lines listed below, be honest with yourself, and write some of the ways you can be self absorbed. Then write some ways you can check yourself when you realize you are doing this. As you move into the Closing Prayer, you may need to ask God for help in this area and forgiveness for the ways you have been arrogant, flirty or tried to draw attention to yourself. God will help you with this if you truly seek Him.

Closing 3:16 Prayer

Heavenly Father,

I bow my head and ask forgiveness for the times I have been like the daughters of Zion. Thank You for restoring me to You and I pray that You will clearly show me when I am beginning to act in ways that do not please You.

In Jesus' name I pray,

Amen

Jeremiah 3:16 NLT

"And when your land is once more filled with people," says the Lord, "you will no longer wish for 'the good old days' when you possessed the Ark of the Lord's Covenant. You will not miss those days or even remember them, and there will be no need to rebuild the Ark."

Jeremiah 3:16 NLT

3:16 Biblical Context

Timeline of Jeremiah 3:1-2, 3:12-19, 3:22, 4:1-4

- ✧ **Jeremiah 3:1-2** – Jeremiah has been called by God to prophesy to Israel and Judah for their continued failings. These first 2 verses pose questions asking if it is possible to return after a separation.
- ✧ **Jeremiah 3:12-14** – God sends Jeremiah to call for Israel to return to Him.
- ✧ **Jeremiah 3:15-19** – If Israel will return and repent from their disobedience, God will bless His people.
- ✧ **Jeremiah 3:22** – God again, summons Judah and Israel to return.
- ✧ **Jeremiah 4:1-4** – This passage closes with Gods final call for Israel and Judah to dedicate themselves or God's anger will consume them.

EXPLORING Jeremiah 3:16

This 3:16 and the chapter surrounding it, give hope for wayward Israel, who has once again fallen away. Chronologically speaking, Jeremiah was originally sent by God to prophesy to Israel & warn Judah of what was to come during King Josiah's reign.

Unfortunately, this happens in our lives as well. You may currently be in a season of your life where you are not reading the Bible consistently, not praying, not listening to God because you have sin that you are not ready to let go of yet. If you aren't in a place where you have fallen away from God, perhaps reading Jeremiah's imploring words from the Lord will help you remember to pray for those that have.

Reading this passage in Jeremiah 3:14-16 reminds us of how God's patience with us draws us back into a right relationship with Him.

> "Come back to Me, my wayward children," says the Lord "for I am your true master. If you do, I will take one of you from each town and two of you from each family group, and I will bring you back to Zion. I will give you leaders who will be faithful to Me. They will lead you with knowledge and insight. And when your land is once more filled with people," says the Lord, "you will no longer wish for 'the good old days' when you possessed the Ark of the Lord's Covenant. You will not miss those days or even remember them, and there will be no need to rebuild the Ark."
>
> Jeremiah 3:14-16

Even now, in our fallen world, God calls His people back to Him. God's patience is everlasting, and He is always waiting to welcome us back.

3:16 Reflect & Connect

Spend some time acknowledging the areas that you struggle with, and make note of those below. If you feel comfortable writing down what you need to work on to get back into a right relationship with the Lord, then write that on the lines below.

____

____

____

____

Now make a list of some of the attributes of God that you connect with. During your closing prayer, thank God for all that He is to you, using the attributes of God that mean the most to you.

____

____

____

____

Closing 3:16 Prayer

Heavenly Father,

Your patience with me is overwhelming. I come to You asking for Your help in the areas I struggle with in my life __________________. God I praise You that Your love for me never changes and for the unmerited favor You continually show me.

In Jesus' name I pray,

Amen

Lamentations 3:16 NLT

He has made me chew on gravel. He has rolled me in the dust.

Lamentations 3:16 NLT

3:16 Biblical Context

Timeline of Lamentations 3:1-66
Lamentation spoken by one Israelite man

- ✧ **Lamentations 3:1-20** – The suffering and despair of Israel.
- ✧ **Lamentations 3:21-33** – Hope in God's faithfulness.
- ✧ **Lamentations 3:34-42** – A call to Israel to reflect and repent.
- ✧ **Lamentations 3:43-66** – A plea for God's intervention.

"The thought of my suffering and homelessness is bitter beyond words. I will never forget this awful time, as I grieve over my loss."
Lamentations 3:19-20 NLT

Exploring Lamentations 3:16

Lamentations is a series of poems, written as prayers to God during a time of grief. Jerusalem had been destroyed and the Israelites taken into captivity by Babylon. The book of Lamentations shows their grief.

Lamentations 3 is a poem which could be titled "one man's complaint". The writer is Jeremiah and Chapter 3 is his personal lament. Jeremiah's solution to Judah's judgment and the fall of the city was to repent and keep their eyes focused on God for restoration.

This 3:16 is such a visual verse. The suffering and the despair being felt by Israel must've been horrible. Repentance is hard as noted by the examples given here of chewing on gravel or being rolled in the dust. Yet, even through all the misery, the lamenter finds *hope* in his darkness,

> "Yet I still dare to hope... The faithful love of the Lord never ends! His mercies never cease. Great is His faithfulness..."
>
> Lamentations 3:21a, 22-23

> "For no one is abandoned by the Lord forever. Though He brings grief, He also shows compassion because of the greatness of His unfailing love."
>
> Lamentations 3:31-33

Just a few verses past this, there is *comfort.*

> "But I called on Your name, Lord, from deep within the pit. "You heard me when I cried, Listen to my pleading~ Hear my cry for help!" Yes You came when I called; You told me "Do not fear". Lord You have come to my defense; You have redeemed my life."
>
> Lamentations 3:55 – 58

3:16 Reflect & Connect

So if you find yourself in a time of chewing on gravel and rolling in the dust, do not fear, this season will pass. Lean into the Lord, read His scripture, and feel the comfort that comes from a renewed relationship with Christ.

The well known hymn, "Great is Thy Faithfulness" by Thomas Chisolm, was inspired by the words found in Lamentations 3. He wrote this poem during a season of his life when he was experiencing declining health, yet

Chisolm never wavered in his acknowledgement of God's provision and faithfulness.

For today's Bible journaling activity, find the song *Great is Thy Faithfulness* and write the lyrics here.

____

____

____

____

____

____

____

____

Great is Thy Faithfulness

Closing 3:16 Prayer

Heavenly Father,

You see my tears and I bring my laments to You. God, I ask that You show me a way out of my grief. Lord, I bring this situation to You for Your healing ______________________. I also bring You the source of my grief _______________ knowing You will work things out for my good.

In Jesus' name I pray,

Amen.

Ezekiel 3:16 NLT

After seven days the Lord gave me a message. He said,
Ezekiel 3:16 NLT

3:16 Biblical Context

Timeline of Ezekiel 3:1-17

- **Ezekiel 3:1-4** – Ezekiel is instructed by God to eat a scroll, and then go give the message to the people of Israel.
- **Ezekiel 3:5-8** – Ezekiel is told that the people of Israel will be difficult to speak to because they are hard headed, stubborn and unwilling to listen to the Lord.
- **Ezekiel 3:9-11** – God says do not be afraid of them but tells Ezekiel to speak the words the Lord gives him.
- **Ezekiel 3:12-15** – God physically moves Ezekiel to the place where these people are and Ezekiel is overwhelmed and sits among the other Judean exiles for 7 days.
- **Ezekiel 3: 16-17** – Ezekiel is appointed a Watchman for Israel and tasked with passing God's warnings on to the Judean exiles.

Exploring Ezekiel 3:16

For a bit of background to help understand what's going on in this 3:16, in Ezekiel 1-3:15, Ezekiel has a vision, and in it God gave him a scroll to eat.

Ezekiel is then told that he will be delivering God's messages to his people, the Judean exiles. God also informs Ezekiel that they are hard headed & hard hearted, and won't listen to Ezekiel any more than they listen to Him. God let Ezekiel know that He would open Ezekiel's mouth and give him the words to speak, yet Ezekiel had to be willing to say those words and allow God's message to be heard.

Something to Think About

God is willing to make Ezekiel a Watchman for Israel, giving them one more chance to repent. God knows they won't listen or repent, but He still gives them the opportunity.

Isn't God's love amazing?

3:16 Reflect & Connect

This passage is given to Ezekiel and it includes his call from God and his commission to give God's message to the Judean exiles. As Christians, we are also called to go and tell others the good news of salvation.

You have a salvation story to tell, write your story of good news here. After you write your salvation story, think of people that you should share it with and write their name(s) at the bottom.

Closing 3:16 Prayer

Heavenly Father,

I live among people who do not know You and I ask You to help me use my story to bring others to You. Lord, I ask that You help open my mouth to speak to ____________ about You. I thank You in advance for the opportunities You will give me.

In Jesus' name I pray,

Amen

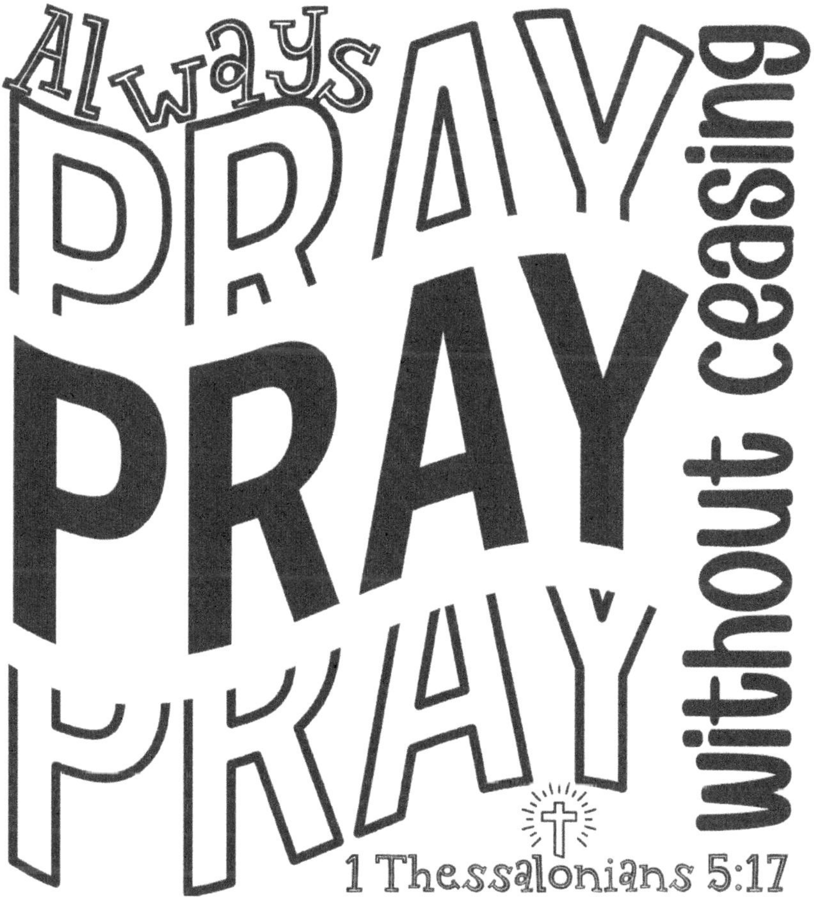

Daniel 3:16 NIV

Shadrach, Meshach, and Abednego replied, "O King Nebuchadnezzar, we do not need to defend ourselves before you in this matter.

Daniel 3:16 NIV

3:16 Biblical Context

Timeline of Daniel 3:1-29

- **Daniel 3:1-7** – King Nebuchadnezzar builds a statue and commands that when the music is played that everyone must bow down to the statue.
- **Daniel 3:8-15** – The astrologers notice that Shadrach, Meshach and Abednego are not bowing and bring this to the King's attention. King Nebuchadnezzar is furious and brings them in to find out if this is true, and gives them a chance to bow down or be thrown in the fire.
- **Daniel 3:16-18** – They do not answer the King's first question, they state that their God is able to rescue them from the fire. They also let the King know that even if God chooses not to save them from the fire, they will never bow down to anyone other than God.
- **Daniel 3:19-25** – Shadrach, Meshach and Abednego are thrown into the fire and not consumed by the flames. It is noticed that a 4th man is in the fire with them.
- **Daniel 3:26-29** – King Nebuchadnezzar has them removed from the fire and sees that they are perfectly fine. The King questions them about how this is possible and they proclaim what their God has done. King Nebuchadnezzar begins to praise God and decrees that no one could say anything against their God.

EXPLORING Daniel 3:16

Shadrach, Meshach and Abednego, may be familiar to those of you who grew up in church. These 3 young men would not bow down and worship the King's gold statue, and in a fit of jealousy, the King threw them in a fiery furnace. This kiln-furnace that the King ordered them to be thrown in, would have been heated from below with charcoal. The King ordered it to be 7 times hotter than usual, and a ramp built so he could watch the 3 men being thrown in. This perfect vantage point that the King used to watch the 3 men burn, instead gave him a clear view of the 4th man, whom he said "looked like a son of the gods." God saved them, and when they came out of the fire, not even their clothes smelled of smoke. The only thing that had been burned away were the ropes used to bind them.

In many countries around the world, standing up for your faith in God can have life threatening consequences, while those in the United States are free to worship how they like. If you live in a place where your right to worship how you choose is protected, it may be hard to understand how you can apply this biblical story to your daily life?

Many times, following Christ means you do not get invited to a party, or do not get asked out by the person you are interested in, because they don't want to date someone who goes to church. These slights, dismissals, or snubs, based solely on your faith, are ways that we can use the story of Shadrach, Meshach and Abednego to encourage us to stand strong in our faith.

3:16 Reflect & Connect

For our Bible journaling activity today, please write down some ways you have been persecuted for your faith.

How did your persecution affect your response to the person, people, or situation in which you were persecuted?

If you didn't handle yourself well in that situation, write down some things you wish you had said or done.

Closing 3:16 Prayer

Heavenly Father,

There are so many places in this world where people are not free to worship You openly. I pray now for those countries who are currently closed to Your gospel and I trust that You can make a way for those people to come to know You.

In Jesus' name I pray,

Amen

Joel 3:16 NLT

The Lord's voice will roar from Zion and thunder from Jerusalem, and the heavens and the earth will shake. But the Lord will be a refuge for his people, a strong fortress for the people of Israel.

Joel 3:16 NLT

3:16 Biblical Context

Timeline of Joel 1-3

- ✧ **Joel 1** – Peril, destruction, mourning and suffering have come to the land, and Joel leads Israel in repentance.
- ✧ **Joel 2** – Descriptions of the Day of the Lord.
- ✧ **Joel 3** – Judgment for the wicked and salvation for the righteous.

Exploring Joel 3:16

The theme of the book of Joel is *The Day of the Lord*. The 3 short chapters, written by Joel, differ from the other 8 Old Testament prophets who wrote about the doom and destruction of the approaching *Day of the Lord*. Joel focused on the time just before and just after the *Day of the Lord*, focusing on the prosperity and blessings awaiting believers.

Within this 3:16, God is portrayed as a *refuge* and a *strong fortress* for His people. This reflects God's promise to protect and provide security for His chosen people. This verse gives us a broader understanding of God's covenant relationship with all who follow Him.

Joel goes on to say that on that day, the mountains will drip with sweet wine, the hills will flow with milk and the streams will fill with fresh water. The book of Joel continues to reaffirm the covenant that Gods' people have with Him. The apostle Paul spelled it out best when he said that both

> "Jew and Gentile are the same in this respect. They have the same Lord, who gives generously to all who call on Him. "Everyone who calls on the name of the Lord will be saved.""
>
> Romans 10:12-13

In today's world, many people feel uncertain about what is to come. Whether that is the end of their life, or the end times when Jesus will return and call His people home. Believers can find comfort in God as their *refuge* and *strong fortress*, experiencing His protection, guidance, and peace as they face life's uncertainties. The book of Joel helps us to keep our eyes on the fact that God is our comfort and protection in uncertain times.

3:16 Reflect & Connect

This 3:16 tells us that the Lord will be a *refuge* and a *strong fortress* for His people. Write synonyms to these words on the lines below. Circle the ones that resonate with you. Thank God for being those things in your life.

Refuge ______________________________

____

____

____

Strong Fortress ______________________________

____

____

____

Closing 3:16 Prayer

Heavenly Father,

As I look at the words I have written, I praise You for being those things in my life. During times of bitterness and in times of blessing, You are my refuge. God I praise You now with the words I circled that best describe who You are in my life_______________,

In Jesus' name I pray,

Amen

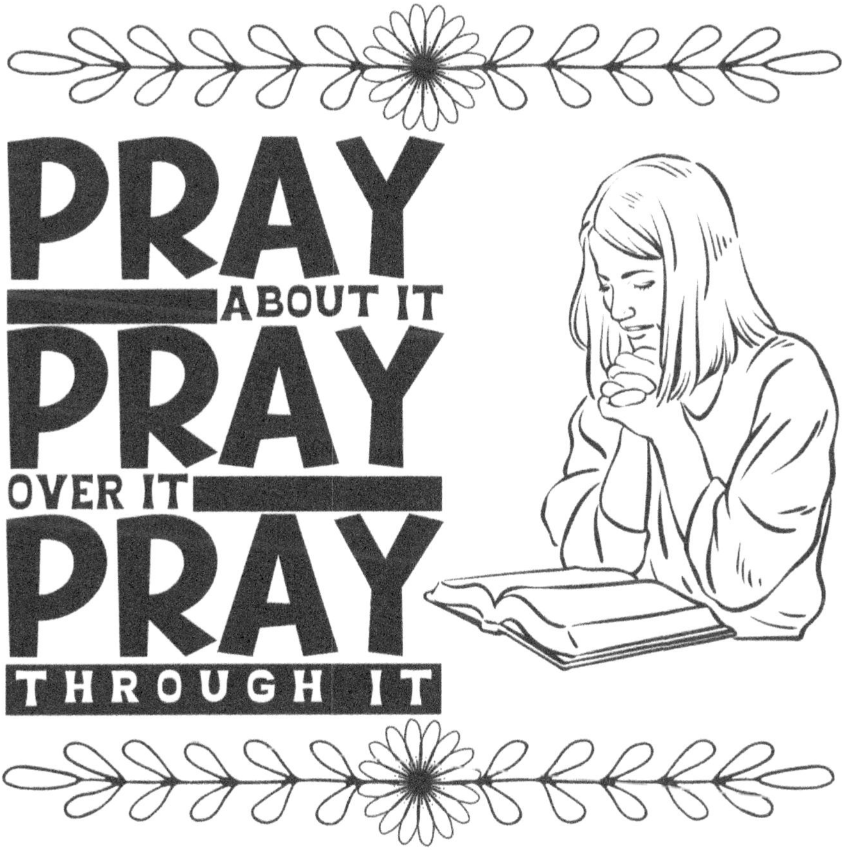

Nahum 3:16 NLT

Your merchants have multiplied until they outnumber the stars. But like a swarm of locusts, they strip the land and fly away.

Nahum 3:16 NLT

3:16 Biblical Context

Timeline of Nahum 1:1-3:16

- **Nahum 1: 1-15** – The Lord is angry with Nineveh because of their defiance.
- **Nahum 2: 1-13** – The siege and fall of Nineveh.
- **Nahum 3: 1-19** – The Lord judges Nineveh.

Exploring Nahum 3:16

This 3:16 is part of the Lord's judgment against Nineveh, the capital of Assyria. You will be familiar with Nineveh if you know the story of Jonah, who called for Nineveh to repent. Nineveh did repent and was spared, unfortunately that repentance did not hold true. Nahum is now being called by God to go to Nineveh and preach repentance for their wicked ways.

The book of Nahum is not filled with positive and uplifting verses. This is a book of judgment for those who oppose the Lord. Nahum tells us that

> "The Lord is a jealous God filled with vengeance and rage. He takes revenge on all who oppose Him and continues to rage against his enemies! The Lord is slow to get angry, but His power is great and He never lets the guilty go unpunished."
>
> Nahum 1:2-3a

God is bringing down His wrath on the Assyrians to "break the yoke of bondage from His people and tear off the chains of Assyrian oppression. (1:13)" Though Assyria "has destroyed Judah, the Lord will restore its honor. Israel's vine has been stripped of branches but He will restore its splendor. (2:2)"

Today's 3:16 highlights the futility of Nineveh's material prosperity in the face of God's judgment. The city's wealth, alliances, and perceived strength cannot save it from its destruction.

The book of Nahum has a total of 47 verses and all but one are focused on the punishment, destruction and doom of Nineveh. Let's close this exploration of Nahum with the one source of comfort in the book:

The Lord is good, a strong refuge when trouble comes. He is close to those who trust in Him.

Nahum 1:7 NLT

While Nahum declares God's wrath against Nineveh, this verse reassures believers that God's justice is paired with goodness and protection for those who seek refuge in Him. As believers and children of God, this verse is comforting. All the judgment and anger that God shows to Nineveh can remind us that God will not allow evil to win.

3:16 Reflect & Connect

In your life, have there been times when you found comfort when witnessing God's judgement of the guilty? Have there been other times, you knowingly disobeyed, hoping that God would not notice? Journal the things that God brought to your mind as you have studied the book of Nahum and thought about judgement.

Write Nahum 1:7 in the space provided below, and really think about what this verse says about our Lord.

Now make a border and decorate around the verse with stickers, doodles and colored pencils, repeating the words of Nahum 1:7 over and over again to help it stick in your memory.

Closing 3:16 Prayer

Heavenly Father,

As I learn more about Your Word, I feel ________________. With this knowledge, allow me to ______________

In Jesus' name I pray,

Amen

Habakkuk 3:16 NLT

I trembled inside when I heard this; my lips quivered with fear. My legs gave way beneath me, and I shook in terror. I will wait quietly for the coming day when disaster will strike the people who invade us.

Habakkuk 3:16 NLT

3:16 Biblical Context

Timeline of Habakkuk 3:1-19

✧ **Habakkuk 3:1-2** – Habakkuk's prayer for revival.
✧ **Habakkuk 3:3-15** – Habakkuk's vision of God's power.
✧ **Habakkuk 3:16-19** – Habakkuk's response of fear and faith.

Exploring Habakkuk 3:16

Habakkuk 3 is a powerful chapter where the prophet transitions from questioning God, to embracing the task God has assigned him to do.

This chapter begins with a prayer in which Habakkuk acknowledges God's mighty works throughout history and pleads for Him to revive them in Habakkuk's time. Habakkuk, although scared, trusts in the Lord even when he can't see the outcome. Finally, Habakkuk sings his prayer, acknowledging God as a mighty warrior and sovereign Lord. This final prayer reflects a deep understanding that God's plans are far greater than human comprehension, and that His mercy is always present, even in the midst of discipline.

Verses 3-15 provide a poetic and vivid depiction of God's majestic power. Drawing from Israel's history, Habakkuk recalls events like the Exodus as well as God's deliverance of His people. The imagery of nature trembling before God, highlights His dominion over all creation, reinforcing the message that no force can stand against Him. This section serves as a reminder that the same God who acted powerfully in the past remains faithful and will act again to deliver and restore His people.

This 3:16 shifts this song of prayer to Habakkuk's personal response. The prophet trembles with fear and awe at the vision of God's judgment and timing. He expresses a willingness to wait patiently, even as disaster approaches. This leads Habakkuk to declare his faith despite his fear and find strength in God alone.

> "Yet I will rejoice in the Lord! I will be joyful in the God of my salvation! And The Sovereign Lord is my strength. He makes me as surefooted as a deer, able to tread upon the heights."
> Habakkuk 3:18-19 NLT

3:16 Reflect & Connect

Reflect on some of the words or phrases in Habakkuk 3:16-19 that speak to you.

> *[16] I trembled inside when I heard this; my lips quivered with fear. My legs gave way beneath me, and I shook in terror. I will wait quietly for the coming day when disaster will strike the people who invade us.[17] Even though the fig trees have no blossoms, and there are no grapes on the vines; even though the olive crop fails, and the fields lie empty and barren; even though the flocks die in the fields, and the cattle barns are empty,[18] yet I will rejoice in the Lord! I will be joyful in the God of my salvation![19] The Sovereign Lord is my strength! He makes me as surefooted as a deer, able to tread upon the heights.*
> Habakkuk 3:16-19 NLT

Use the lines provided to pour out your praise to God for His Holiness, Might and Power.

Closing 3:16 Prayer

Heavenly Father,

I have written words that show the awe I have for You. Lord, I praise You for creating me in Your image and I make a commitment to You to continue to seek more ways to be like You each day.

In Jesus' name I pray,

Amen

PRAY

Zephaniah 3:16 NLT

On that day the announcement to Jerusalem will be, "Cheer up, Zion! Don't be afraid!

Zephaniah 3:16 NLT

3:16 Biblical Context

Timeline of Zephaniah 3:14-17

- ✧ **Zephaniah 3:14** – God's people are told to rejoice.
- ✧ **Zephaniah 3:15** – God is done with His judgment, and reigns as their King.
- ✧ **Zephaniah 3:16** – God reassures His people not to fear, as He is in their midst.
- ✧ **Zephaniah 3:17** – God delights in His people, bringing calm with His love.

Exploring Zephaniah 3:16

Zephaniah was a prophet who lived in Jerusalem. He was the great-great-grandson of King Hezekiah. Being of Royal descent, Zephaniah would have been uniquely positioned to speak boldly to the wealthy city of Jerusalem about their spiritual and political corruption. not to mention his warning of the coming "*Day of the Lord*" and call to repent.

This 3:16 comes from the part of Zephaniah's prophecy that brings hope to not only the people of Israel & Judah, but to all nations. The remnant of God's people are called to rejoice because He has removed their judgment, defeated their enemies, and promised His presence among them. Emphasizing God's love, protection, and joy over His people. Painting a picture of restoration and hope, where fear and shame are replaced with peace and celebration. God is depicted not only as a mighty warrior who saves but also as a loving father who delights in His children.

This also offers hope for believers as it assures us of God's plan to bring restoration, peace, and joy to His people. While this prophecy awaits future fulfillment, it reminds us today of God's character—He is a loving and faithful God who delights in His people. For Christians, this points to the assurance we have in Jesus Christ, whose return will usher in the fulfillment of these promises. It encourages us to live with faith and anticipation, knowing that God's salvation and joy will ultimately be fully realized.

3:16 Reflect & Connect

Imagine that Zephaniah was calling out to you, what would his message be, specifically to you? What area of your life would he tell you to rejoice and not be afraid? Fill in those answers into the lines listed below.

Closing 3:16 Prayer

Heavenly Father,

Help me to seek comfort in You rather than the things of this world. Lord, I am in a time of ____________ in my life and I ask You to be close to me and guide me with Your wisdom as You guided the people of Jerusalem.

In Jesus' name I pray.

Amen

Malachi 3:16 NIV

Then those who feared the Lord talked with each other, and the Lord listened and heard. A scroll of remembrance was written in His presence concerning those who feared the Lord and honored His name.

Malachi 3:16 NIV

3:16 Biblical Context

Timeline of Malachi 2:10-3:18

- **Malachi 2:10-16** – This passage condemns Judah's dishonesty and faithlessness
- **Malachi 3:1-6** – This passage speaks of a time of purification and judgment handed down from the Lord's messenger
- **Malachi 3:7-15** – Call to return to God and stop robbing Him
- **Malachi 3:16-18** – God's greatness is shown to a repentant Judah and the distinction between the righteous and the wicked.

Exploring Malachi 3:16

The book of Malachi, the final book of the Old Testament, is a prophetic message to the post Babylonian Israelites. Malachi addresses the Israelites spiritual apathy, and calls them back to faithfulness. God exposes the people's sins and reassures them of His justice and love.

This 3:16 is part of the last dispute where God accuses Israel of speaking arrogantly against Him. This is the dispute that divides the wicked from the faithful. A scroll of remembrance was written in God's presence concerning those who feared the Lord and honored His name.

This is a hopeful verse for those priests and people of Israel who have remained faithful. God promised to remember their faithfulness. Such an empowering verse for those who remain righteous. Those Israelites who received this promise that God would remember them, would finish out their lives trusting this promise, sharing it with their children and grandchildren, creating a legacy of faithfulness.

This 3:16 reminds us of two things that Christians need to keep at the forefront of our minds.

✦ We as believers need to listen and speak to other believers. This can keep us from going astray, and help us during times when we do not know how to move forward.

✦ We need to remain faithful, fearing the Lord and honoring His name.

Something to Think About

The Lord of Heaven's Armies–Jehovah Sabaoth–is mentioned 21 times in Malachi, a reminder of God's power and sovereignty.

Are you trusting in His strength to face life's battles?

3:16 Reflect & Connect

Spend some time thinking about which of these two ways you need to be more faithful. Write or draw in each letter of the word FAITHFUL some specific examples of ways that you will begin to be more FAITHFUL to the Lord this week.

FAITHFUL

Closing 3:16 Prayer

Heavenly Father,

I commit today to be more faithful to You in the area(s) of _____________. I also ask You to help me begin to read Your word more consistently so that I can better understand Your will for my life.

In Jesus' name I pray,

Amen

Matthew 3:16 NLT

After his baptism, as Jesus came up out of the water, the heavens were opened and he saw the Spirit of God descending like a dove and settling on Him.

Matthew 3:16 NLT

3:16 Biblical Context

Timeline of Matthew 3:1-17

- ✧ **Matthew 3:1-6** – John the Baptist, a preacher, was baptizing folks from around Judea in the Jordan river and preaching about the Messiah who was coming.
- ✧ **Matthew 3:7-12** – John denounced the Pharisees and Sadducees, warning them of God's coming judgment.
- ✧ **Matthew 3:14-17** – Jesus comes to John and asks to be baptized. When he came up out of the water, the Spirit of God descended upon Him.

Exploring Matthew 3:16

Baptism is a public profession of an inward commitment to God. It is not required to become a Christian, however, Jesus led by example and was baptized. When Jesus approached John the Baptist and asked to be baptized, John originally hesitated, he knew Jesus was sinless, and John felt unworthy to baptize Jesus.

Matthew 3:15 is Jesus's response to John, if we look at several different Biblical translations, we get a well rounded understanding of what Jesus was asking of John.

"It should be done, for we must carry out all that God requires." NLT

"Let it be so now; it is proper for us to do this to fulfill all righteousness." NIV

"Suffer *it to be so* now: for thus it becometh us to fulfill all righteousness." KJV

"Permit *it to be so* now, for thus it is fitting for us to fulfill all righteousness." NKJV

"For now this is how it should be, because we must do all God wants us to do." CEV

This 3:16 tells us that, "as Jesus came up out of the water, the heavens were opened and He saw the Spirit of God descending like a dove and settling on Him." Verse17 finishes the scene, "And a voice from heaven said, "This is My dearly loved Son, who brings Me great joy.""

Passages of Scripture like this, make it obvious that God's ways are not our ways. God set this into motion in Isaiah 40:3-5, roughly 700 years before, when He told us one who would come shouting in the wilderness (John the Baptist) would fulfill the prophecy, just as the Lord had commanded it, paving the way for Jesus. As followers of Christ, we should follow the example of our risen Savior into baptism.

3:16 Reflect & Connect

If you have not been baptized, talk with a leader at your church. If you have, write in this journal about that day in your life. Once you have written it, consider sharing it with someone in your life this week. It may be just the thing needed to help someone recognize their need for the Lord.

____

____

____

____

____

____

Share your FAITH

Closing 3:16 Prayer

Heavenly Father,

I praise You for Your saving grace and the opportunity to know You as my personal Savior. Lord, I ask that You bring someone into my life who needs to hear about You and that You will give me an opportunity to talk to them in the near future.

In Jesus' name I pray,

Amen

Mark 3:16 NIV

These are the twelve he appointed: Simon (to whom he gave the name Peter),

Mark 3:16 NIV

3:16 Biblical Context

Timeline of Mark 3:13-19

- **Mark 3:13-15** – Jesus has begun His ministry and is prepared to choose 12 men to serve alongside Him in His ministry.
- **Mark 3:16-19** – Jesus calls His 12 disciples.

Exploring Mark 3:16

In Mark chapter 3, we see that Jesus has begun His ministry and in Mark 3:16-19, we see Him call the 12 men who will be His disciples. These men came from various backgrounds and each were selected to fulfill God's ultimate plan.

Which of the disciples are easiest for you to remember? Perhaps John the disciple who was the one whom Jesus loved like a brother? Maybe it's Peter, who had a bold faith that allowed him to walk on water until he took his eyes off of Jesus? What about poor Thomas, who will forever be immortalized as, "doubting Thomas" because he refused to believe in the resurrection until he could see and touch Jesus' wounds for himself? Or is it, Judas, the betrayer, who sold Jesus out for 30 pieces of silver?

It can be hard to understand why Jesus would choose someone who He knew would betray Him. Judas was the treasurer of the group, he would have been highly regarded among the disciples and Jesus gave him the seat of honor at the last supper.

If we had this foreknowledge, we would never have chosen someone who would hurt us. However, Jesus chose him, because Judas's actions led to several Old Testament prophecies being fulfilled. Which serves as a reminder that God's ways are not our ways.

John 3:16 Correlation: Jesus' sacrifice on the cross was for all.

- ✦ Those who serve Him faithfully all the days of their lives like John (the disciple that Jesus loved like a brother)
- ✦ Those who love the Lord yet fail in big ways like Peter
- ✦ Those who proclaim Him publicly yet inwardly are traitors, hypocrites and betrayers like Judas.

It is not our decision to determine who is worthy of Heaven, it is our mission to bring as many to the cross as possible and allow them an opportunity to come to know our risen Lord Jesus.

In John 3:16, God loved the whole world and sent His Son to offer eternal life to everyone who chooses to follow Him. Together these verses show God's love both personally and universally––calling individuals, like Peter, and offering salvation to all through Jesus.

3:16 Reflect & Connect

Use the lines below to name all 12 disciples? If you need a little help, you can find their names in Mark 3:16-19

1. ______________________
2. ______________________
3. ______________________
4. ______________________
5. ______________________
6. ______________________
7. ______________________
8. ______________________
9. ______________________
10. ______________________
11. ______________________
12. ______________________

Closing 3:16 Prayer

Heavenly Father,

Thank You for calling me to be Your child. Thank You for the assurance that I can trust You in all ways. In this fallen world, not everyone is worthy of trust. Right now Lord I pray for those who have been betrayed, and ask that You begin to heal that hurt, and teach them how to forgive their betrayers, because that forgiveness will help heal them as well.

If this situation applies directly to you:

There have been times when someone has betrayed my trust, and the hurt from that betrayal weighs heavily on me. God, I ask that You begin to heal that hurt. (Spend some additional time praying more deeply about your situation.)

Lord, I also pray for the people who have been the betrayer, and ask that You would touch their lives and help them see the error of their ways. Please help them come to a saving knowledge of You.

In Jesus' name I pray,

Amen

Luke 3:16 NLT

John answered their questions by saying, "I baptize you with water; but someone is coming soon who is greater than I am—so much greater that I'm not even worthy to be his slave and untie the straps of his sandals. He will baptize you with the Holy Spirit and with fire.

Luke 3:16 NLT

3:16 Biblical Context

Timeline of Luke 3:2b-18

- **Luke 3:2b-14** – A message from God came to John so he spoke to the people throughout the regions of the Jordan River, preaching the Gospel and baptizing people.
- **Luke 3:15** – The people were amazed with what John said and began to wonder if John was the Messiah.
- **Luke 3:16-18** – John addressed the people and clearly defines that he is not the Messiah, just a messenger of the One who is to come.

Exploring Luke 3:16

The ministry of John, known as John the Baptist, was to point others to the coming Messiah, as was prophesied by Isaiah roughly 700 years ago. John was an evangelical preacher, who met people where they were. His messages were practical and paved the way for the coming Messiah.

It's not surprising that people might have begun to think that John was the Messiah. In verses 3:16-18 we see John's humility as he clarifies that he is not the Messiah, and goes on to say he is not worthy to untie the straps of the Messiah's sandals.

John 3:16 correlation: In Luke 3:16, John the Baptist was responsible for preaching the gospel and baptizing new believers. This format of hearing the word of God and responding to its free gift is the exact format laid out in the second half of John 3:16 where we read that everyone who believes in Him shall receive eternal life.

Luke 3:16 also speaks of the baptism of the Holy Spirit and John 3:16 is that fulfillment in our lives.

3:16 Reflect & Connect

This verse shows us an empowered Christian life. A life in which the Holy Spirit empowers us to live boldly for God. When someone gives their life to Christ, they are baptized in the Holy Spirit.

If you have not given your life to Christ, consider doing that today, then share your decision with your church leader, and journal your decision on the lines below. (A simple prayer of salvation is located at the end of this journal).

If you are a Christian write about a time when you clearly remember the Holy Spirit being present in your life.

Closing 3:16 Prayer

Heavenly Father,

I praise You for John the Baptist who proclaimed Your word to people so they had the opportunity to come to Christ. I thank You that ____________________shared the Gospel with me. Lord, I ask that You allow the Holy Spirit to work mightily in my life so that I may speak boldly when You give me opportunities.

In Jesus' name I pray,

Amen

John 3:16 NIV

"For God so loved the world that He gave his one and only Son, that whoever believes in Him shall not perish but have eternal life."

John 3:16 NIV

3:16 Biblical Context

Timeline of John 3:1-21

- **John 3:1-2** – Nicodemus, a Pharisee, visits Jesus at night, acknowledging Him as a teacher from God.
- **John 3:3-8** – Jesus teaches Nicodemus about being born again.
- **John 3:9-15** – Nicodemus struggles to understand. Jesus questions why Nicodemus and others who follow the law still do not believe what they have seen. Jesus speaks of His authority to teach these truths.
- **John 3:16-18** – Jesus tells Nicodemus that God didn't send His Son to condemn the world, but to save it through Him.
- **John 3:19-21** – Jesus shares the path to Heaven for those who will believe.

Exploring John 3:16

A Pharisee named Nicodemus came to have a conversation with Jesus late one evening. Being a member of the Jewish ruling council, Nicodemus knew who Jesus was and sought Him out. Nicodemus starts by flattering Jesus, saying, "Rabbi, we know that You are a teacher who has come from God. For no one could perform the miracles You are doing if God were not with Him." Jesus tells Nicodemus that "only those born again can see the Kingdom of God."

This seems like an odd reply. It's almost as if Jesus was replying to Nicodemus's soul, rather than his words. Whether Nicodemus sought out

Jesus from his own curiosity, or was sent by the other religious leaders, it's obvious that Nicodemus wasn't prepared for what Jesus had to say to him. The Pharisee couldn't comprehend how someone could be born again.

Jesus' answer, that "flesh gives birth to flesh, but the Spirit gives birth to spirit" just confuses Nicodemus and he asks, "How can this be?" Jesus explains that even though you have heard the truth and seen the miracles, you still choose not to believe. "How then will you believe if I speak of heavenly things?"

This night time conversation with Nicodemus concludes with verses 3:16-21, where the plan of salvation is laid out for those who choose to believe.

3:16 Reflect & Connect

We have finally arrived at the most recognized verse in the entire Bible. Spend some time coloring the next page to help you focus on these well known words.

Closing 3:16 Prayer

Heavenly Father,

Your Word is such a blessing in my life. Thank You for giving me the Bible so that I can know You better. Lord, I know that You loved the world so much that You gave Your one and only Son so that everyone who believes in Him will not perish but have everlasting life. Lord, I praise You that by putting my faith in Jesus, I get to spend eternity with You. Please give me the opportunity to share this good news with others, so they can know of this gift You have given us.

In Jesus' name I pray,

Amen

FOR
GOD SO LOVED
the WORLD
THAT HE gave HIS
ONE & ONLY
SON That Whoever BELIEVES
IN HIM NOT Perish
but have
Everlasting LIFE.
John 3:16

Acts 3:16 NLT

"Through faith in the name of Jesus, this man was healed—and you know how crippled he was before. Faith in Jesus' name has healed him before your very eyes."

Acts 3:16 NLT

3:16 Biblical Context

Timeline of Acts 3:1-20

- ✧ **Acts 3:1** – Peter and John were going to the temple for a time of prayer.
- ✧ **Acts 3:2-3** – The area around the temple was often occupied by those with physical ailments who were brought there to beg for money. A man who had been lame since birth was brought to the temple gate where he spoke to Peter and John, asking for money.
- ✧ **Acts 3:4-7** – Peter and John told the man that they didn't have money but they would give him what they did have. They spoke to the man in the name and power of Jesus Christ. They told the man to get up and walk and he was instantly healed.
- ✧ **Acts 3:8-11** – The healed man walked with Peter and John into the temple and people realized that he was the lame man who used to beg at the gate.
- ✧ **Acts 3:12-20** – Word spread of his healing, and people gathered to question Peter and John about the miracle. Peter uses this opportunity to reveal to the crowd that it was God's power working in them to allow the man to be healed. Peter goes on to remind the people that they chose to send Jesus to the cross, however, God will again send Jesus to take his place as Messiah.

EXPLORING Acts 3:16

Jesus, also called, The Great Physician, healed people that He came across in His travels. There are many records of this in the Bible. Jesus also gave that ability to His disciples, as we see in this 3:16, where Peter healed a man who had been lame since birth. The man in Acts 3:16 had a physical disability that was so severe that Peter felt the need to say, "you know how crippled he was before".

Most Biblical scholars agree that Luke was the author of Acts. Luke was also a physician by trade. This is probably why he chose to include the account of the lame man's healing in Acts. The physician in Luke would have been astounded by a man that had been lame since birth becoming instantly healed. God can do things that medical professionals can not.

3:16 Reflect & Connect

This 3:16 may have brought to mind someone in your life who has been healed. If that is the case, in your Closing Prayer today, spend some time praising God for His miraculous gift of healing.

If you know someone in need of healing, please understand that physical healing during their lifetime may not be in God's plan for them. However, our responsibility is to pray and trust God, so ask for His will to be done. You will be able to do this during your Closing Prayer today.

If your loved one is not healed physically or mentally while on this earth. Continue to pray for their salvation, and do what you can to help them become a believer so that they can be assured that they will spend eternity with Christ. In Heaven we all will be healed. Write the name or initials of the person who needs healing here then move on to the Closing Prayer and ask God to do a work in their life.

____

Closing 3:16 Prayer

Heavenly Father,

I lift up _________________ to You. They are in need of physical healing. Father, I know that in You there is healing. Whether You choose to heal them in this lifetime or if Your will is to heal them by bringing them home to You, I trust that You will do what is best for them.

Lord I lift up __________________ to You. They are in need of emotional healing, I ask Lord that Your healing touch will bring comfort and strength to their lives.

Lord I lift up medical professionals and those in counseling professions who are called upon each day to provide aid and comfort to those in need of healing. I praise You for the skills You have blessed them with and I pray You will hold them close as they work to provide help to those in need.

In Jesus' name I pray,

Amen

Romans 3:16 NIV

Ruin and misery lie in their wake,

Romans 3:16 NIV

3:16 Biblical Context

Timeline of Romans 3:9-26

- **Romans 3:9** – Paul is introducing himself to the Roman Christians and he was in Rome to remind them that all Jews and Gentiles have sinned.
- **Romans 3:10-20** – Paul continued writing how people are naturally selfish and prone to sin. No one is righteous.
- **Romans 3:21-26** – Although all have sinned, all can be made right through the sacrifice Christ made on the cross.

Exploring Romans 3:16

Just reading verse 16 may lead you to believe that ruin and misery are waiting for you; however when we widen our focus onto the verses before this 3:16, we see that Paul is answering a question about how all have sinned and Jews' are not better than non-Jews.

If you read Romans 3:10-18 alone, each of those verses seem very bleak and would lead you to hopelessness. It is verse 9 that helps us put into perspective what Paul's true meaning is.

If you continue on in the chapter, you find that verse 22 is the fulfillment of this passage. Righteousness is given through faith in Jesus Christ to everyone (Jew and Gentile) who believes in Him.

EXPLORING Romans 3:16

As you read the entire passage, use the lines after each verse to write a reminder to yourself of how you will follow Jesus rather than be trapped under the power of sin

Example:

10. There is no one righteous, not even one. <u>Jesus is righteous, I will follow His example rather than following the example of any one person.</u>

9."Well then, should we conclude that we Jews are better than others? No, not at all, for we have already shown that all people, whether Jews or Gentiles, are under the power of sin. **10.** There is no one righteous, not even one. ______________________________

____

11. There is no one who understands, no one who seeks God. **12.** All have turned away, they have together become worthless; there is no one who does good, not even one." ______________________________

____

13."Their throats are open graves; their tongues practice deceit." "The venom of vipers is on their lips." **14.**"Their mouths are full of cursing and bitterness." ______________________________

____

15. "Their feet are swift to shed blood; **16.** ruin and misery lie in their wake, ______________________________

____

17. and the way of peace they do not know." **18**. "There is no fear of God before their eyes." ______________________________

____

19. Now we know that whatever the law says, it says to those who are under the law, so that every mouth may be silenced and the whole world held accountable to God. **20**. Therefore no one will be declared righteous in God's sight by the works of the law; rather, through the law we become conscious of our sin. ______________________________

____

21. But now apart from the law the righteousness of God has been made known, to which the Law and the Prophets testify. **22**. This righteousness is given through faith in Jesus Christ to all who believe. There is no difference between Jew and Gentile, ______________________

____

Closing 3:16 Prayer

Heavenly Father,

Romans gave me a strong reminder of how sin can derail my life. Lord, I know You have promised to provide a way out from under temptation and I ask that You give me the strength to walk away from the sin that so easily ensnares me.

In Jesus' name I pray,

Amen

1 Corinthians 3:16 BSB

Do you not know that you yourselves are God's temple, and that God's Spirit dwells in you?
1 Corinthians 3:16 BSB

3:16 Biblical Context

Timeline of 1 Corinthians 3: 1-23

- ✧ **1 Corinthians 3:1-4** – Paul points out the the members of the Church in Corinth are still immature in their faith.
- ✧ **1 Corinthians 3:5-9** – Paul gives numerous reasons why there should not be divisions, rather every person should serve the Lord.
- ✧ **1 Corinthians 3:10-15** – Build the foundation of your life on Jesus Christ.
- ✧ **1 Corinthians 3:16-17** – We are God's temple and we should take good care of His temple.
- ✧ **1 Corinthians 3:18-23** – Wisdom that the world gives is useless. Stop boasting about human leaders.

Exploring 1 Corinthians 3:16

As the Corinthian church had grown, they had become very worldly, relying on human wisdom. They had stopped seeking God's wisdom and were splintering off into different circles of influence.

Paul uses the analogy of babies drinking milk to point out that the Corinthians had been Christians for plenty of time to grow in their faith yet they were still spiritually immature.

Paul gave them several examples to help the members of the church focus on unity in serving Christ, since the Church at Corinth was stuck in divisions over who followed Paul and who followed Apollos. Paul clearly lays out that he and Apollos are merely the tools that God used to bring them to Christ, wisely shifting the attention back to the work the church should be concentrating on which is bringing others to faith in God.

3:16 Reflect & Connect

Get creative with this journaling prompt, you are God's temple where God's Spirit dwells, draw what that looks like to you.

TEMPLE OF THE HOLY SPIRIT

"Your body is the temple of the Holy Spirit who lives in you and was given to you by God. You do not belong to yourself for God bought you with a high price. So you must honor God with your body

1 Corinthians 6:19-20 NLT

Closing 3:16 Prayer

Heavenly Father,

I struggle, like the church in Corinth, with chasing worldly things and dividing my loyalties, which take my focus off of You. I ask that You help me with _______________ which distracts me from what I should be doing. Lord, forgive me for that. I will do my best to remember that I am Your Temple where Your Holy Spirit dwells.

In Jesus' name I pray,

Amen

2 Corinthians 3:16 NIV

But whenever anyone turns to the Lord, the veil is taken away.

2 Corinthians 3:16 NIV

3:16 Biblical Context

Timeline of 2 Corinthians 3:12-18

- **2 Corinthians 3:12-15** – Initial explanation of the difference in someone without faith in Jesus and those with faith in Jesus. Explained using a veil that Moses wore.
- **2 Corinthians 3:16-18** – When someone turns to the Lord, the veil is lifted.

Exploring 2 Corinthians 3:16

Paul had chastised the immaturity of the believers in his previous letter to Corinth, yet in 2 Corinthians, we see a mature church that is standing firm in their faith, and now Paul turns his attention to encouraging the believers to live in unity. In this 3:16 Paul mentions that those who have turned to the Lord have had the veil removed and are able to see clearly the truth of what Jesus did on the cross.

John 3:16 Correlation: In 2 Corinthians 3:16 Paul uses Moses's veil to show the progression from the Old Covenant (law of Moses), to the New Covenant (faith in Jesus Christ) to strengthen the faith of the believers in Corinth.

John 3:16 mirrors the progression from the Old Covenant need to repent from sins with a sacrifice made for those sins with the New Covenant, where the death of Jesus on the cross, made a way for humankind to be reconciled to God through the sacrifice of His son, the spotless lamb. There is no need, under the New Covenant, to sacrifice animals anymore. Jesus's sacrifice paid the price for everyone who believes in Him.

3:16 Reflect & Connect

Sin creates a veil, covering our ability to see God. When someone turns their life to follow God, that veil has been lifted. On the top half of this page, write down a list of people you know that have given their life to the Lord. Spend some time praising God for the people on your list that you are certain will be in Heaven with you

On the bottom half of this page, write down a list of people you know that have not given their lives to the Lord so you can be reminded to pray for them. Spend some time thinking about those in your life who still have that veil over their lives. Your eyes may be drawn to one of those names, if so, circle the name and use the Closing Prayer as a guide to lift that person before God for salvation.

Closing 3:16 Prayer

Heavenly Father,

I pray for ________________ who does not know You. Lord, I know that it is Your desire for all to come to You and I humbly ask that You begin to plow up the hardened ground of their heart and make a way for them to receive Your free gift of eternal salvation. Lord give me the ability to speak into their lives as You give me opportunities. Lord, bring someone into their life who can help them see that this veil is keeping them separated from the true saving power of Jesus Christ.

In Jesus' name I pray,

Amen

Galatians 3:16 NLT

God gave the promises to Abraham and his child. And notice that the Scripture doesn't say 'to his children,' as if it meant many descendants. Rather it says 'to his child' -and that, of course, means Christ.

Galatians 3:16 NLT

3:16 Biblical Context

Timeline of Galatians 3: 15-18

- **Galatians 3:15** – Greeting to brothers and sisters.
- **Galatians 3:16** – Explanation of the promise given to Abraham.
- **Galatians 3:17-18** – Declaration of the unchanging nature of God and the covenant He made with Abraham.

Exploring Galatians 3:16

Paul wrote the book of Galatians to churches throughout Galatia. At the time the amount of Non-Jewish believers was rapidly growing and the different cultures were clashing over practices that were required in the Torah. Jewish believers were arguing that Non-Jewish believers had to follow the practices or they were not true believers. These Jewish believers had caused trouble in the churches in Galatia and Paul's letter was a stern response to those believers who were causing division.

In chapter 3, we see Paul referencing Abraham and the covenant given by God. Paul goes on to share that Jesus, the "child" of Abraham, had fulfilled the requirements of the law and requiring Non-Jewish believers to follow Jewish customs was discrediting what Jesus did on the cross.

3:16 Reflect & Connect

God gave a promise to Abraham so many years ago and today God continues to give good gifts to His children. Some of those things have already come to completion and others are still waiting on an answer.

For the lines on the left, list some of those blessings that you have received from God. For the lines on the right, list the things that you have asked God for that you are still waiting on.

Blessings

Received	**Waiting on**
______________________	______________________
______________________	______________________
______________________	______________________
______________________	______________________
______________________	______________________
______________________	______________________

Now that you are done writing your lists, look at the list on the left, the blessings received. Remember when you were praying for those things, and how it may have felt like they would never happen? Spend some time praising God that they did.

Now look at the things on the list on the right, and commit to trusting God to work how He sees fit. This is so much easier to say than it is to do. So as you move to the Closing Prayer, ask God to build your faith.

Closing 3:16 Prayer

Heavenly Father,

I am in awe of the things You continue to show me in Your word. God I praise You for the blessings You have given me and I pray for wisdom to wait on those things that I am still praying for. Lord guide me in knowing if those are things You desire to give me.

In Jesus' name I pray,

Amen

Ephesians 3:16 BSB

I ask that out of the riches of His glory He may strengthen you with power through His Spirit in your inner being.

Ephesians 3:16 BSB

3:16 Biblical Context

Timeline of Ephesians 3:12 & 3:14-21

- **Ephesians 3:12** – Paul explains to the people that because of the sacrifice of Jesus, we can come directly to God in prayer.
- **Ephesians 3:14-21** – Paul's prayer for the Ephesians.

Exploring Ephesians 3:16

Paul wrote this letter to the church in Ephesus. The goal would have been for the letter he had written to start in Ephesus, then circulate among the other churches in the area. This accounts for Paul's straightforward approach in his wording.

Chapter 3 serves as the conclusion of the first part of this letter. It is in this 3:16, that we see Paul's fervent prayer for God to give them strength through His Spirit. "So that Christ may dwell in their hearts through faith." Paul prayed this so that the Ephesians would comprehend the fullness of Christ's love and be filled with the fullness of God.

3:16 Reflect & Connect

Paul prays at the end of this chapter. This prayer starts in verse 14 and Paul focuses on God's glory, a common theme in Ephesians. Praying scripture back to God can be a powerful way to focus on the Glory of God.

Look at Paul's prayers in Ephesians:

15 For this reason, ever since I heard about your faith in the Lord Jesus and
your love for all the saints, 16 I have not stopped giving thanks for you,
remembering you in my prayers, 17 that the God of our Lord Jesus Christ,
the glorious Father, may give you a spirit of wisdom and revelation in your
knowledge of Him. 18 I ask that the eyes of your heart may be enlightened,
so that you may know the hope of His calling, the riches of His glorious
inheritance in the saints, 19 and the surpassing greatness of His power to
us who believe. These are in accordance with the working of His mighty
strength, 20 which He exerted in Christ when He raised Him from the dead
and seated Him at His right hand in the heavenly realms,

Ephesians 1:15-20 BSB

14 ... for this reason I bow my knees before the Father, 15 from whom every
family in heaven and on earth derives its name. 16 I ask that out of the riches
of His glory He may strengthen you with power through His Spirit in your
inner being, 17 so that Christ may dwell in your hearts through faith. Then
you, being rooted and grounded in love, 18 will have power, together with
all the saints, to comprehend the length and width and height and depth
19 of the love of Christ, and to know this love that surpasses knowledge,
that you may be filled with all the fullness of God. 20 Now to Him who
is able to do so much more than all we ask or imagine, according to His
power that is at work within us, 21 to Him be the glory in the church and
in Christ Jesus throughout all generations, forever and ever. Amen.

Ephesians 3:14-21 BSB

Write the words or phrases Paul used that showed his adoration for God along with the things he was praying for. Use these words or phrases to guide your closing prayer.

Closing 3:16 Prayer

Heavenly Father,

I lift up to You, those words that You drew my attention to in Ephesians. ________________________________, Thank You for showing me these things and giving me an opportunity to pray using Your scripture.

In Jesus' name I pray,
Amen

Philippians 3:16 BSB

Nevertheless, we must live up to what we have already attained.

Philippians 3:16 BSB

3:16 Biblical Context

Timeline of Philippians 3:8-17

- **Philippians 3:8** – Paul speaks about gaining Christ.
- **Philippians 3:9-14** – The benefits of having a personal relationship with Christ.
- **Philippians 3:15-17** – Paul encourages the Philippians to walk as mature believers.

Exploring Philippians 3:16

You know people who are more well read in the Bible than you, as well as people who are just beginning their faith journey and do not know the Bible at all. In this 3:16, Paul is encouraging the Philippians to start where they are, and keep seeking Jesus above all things. We can take this verse and apply it to our lives, not by comparing ourselves to those with more or less knowledge, but rather by living up to what we already know and seeking to become closer to Jesus every day.

3:16 Reflect & Connect

Fill in the sentences with ways you will seek to grow in your faith.

1. I will seek to grow closer to Jesus this week by... ____________________

____

____

2. I will seek to grow closer to Jesus by the end of this study by...__________

____

____

3. I will seek to grow closer to Jesus by this time next year by... __________

____

____

Closing 3:16 Prayer

Heavenly Father,

I come to You now seeking Your wisdom. I have trusted You with my life and I want to seek You more each day. Lord help me to do that by reading Your Word more consistently.

In Jesus' name I pray,
Amen

BUT SEEK FIRST
THE KINGDOM OF GOD
AND HIS RIGHTEOUSNESS,
AND ALL THESE THINGS
WILL BE ADDED UNTO YOU
MATTHEW 6:33

Colossians 3:16 BSB

Let the word of Christ richly dwell within you as you teach and admonish one another with all wisdom, and as you sing psalms, hymns, and spiritual songs with gratitude in your hearts to God.

Colossians 3:16 BSB

3:16 Biblical Context

Timeline of Colossians 3: 12-17

- **Colossians 3:12-17** – Believers are asked to put on compassion, kindness, humility, gentleness, patience, and forgiveness, then step out in love.

Exploring Colossians 3:16

This 3:16 is nestled in the surrounding verses which encourage believers to show compassion, kindness, humility, gentleness, patience and forgiveness. Believers are called to live in peace with one another. These things are difficult to accomplish in today's society with its "me first" mentality.

Considering all that Paul said that believers should be, the church should be a place where these things are readily on display, yet there is a good chance that you know someone who has had a negative experience in church. Some of those experiences have left scars deep enough that they are unwilling to ever step foot inside a church building again. We, being God centered, must begin to show the love of Christ both inside and outside the walls of the church building.

In this 3:16, believers are reminded that Christ dwells in us, and when we teach and correct others, it should be done with wisdom. The verse ends with a reminder to carry our gratitude to God by singing songs that Glorify God. It has never been easier to find songs that Glorify God. Radio stations, podcasts and downloadable music help us to keep gratitude in our hearts to God, which prepares us to live a Christ centered life that will shine like a beacon to a hurting world.

3:16 Reflect & Connect

This 3:16 tells us to sing to the Lord with a grateful heart. Use the lines below to write lyrics from your favorite songs or hymns. If you are able to sing those songs to the Lord today then sing out, God loves to hear you praise Him with song.

Closing 3:16 Prayer

Heavenly Father,

I praise You for music that Glorifies You. I praise You for Christian Artists who sing of Your Love. I come to You today with a song in my heart and I pray that as I go throughout my week, You will provide opportunities for me to show Your love to others around me.

In Jesus' name I pray,

Amen

2 Thessalonians 3:16 NIV

Now may the Lord of peace Himself give you peace at all times and in every way. The Lord be with all of you.
2 Thessalonians 3:16 NIV

3:16 Biblical Context

Timeline of 2 Thessalonians 1- 3:16

- **2 Thessalonians 1-2** – Paul speaking on the return of Christ and reassuring those who were concerned about the time of persecution.
- **2 Thessalonians 3:1- 15** – Paul brings the focus back on proper living.
- **2 Thessalonians 3:16** – Paul's final closing to this book is a word of comfort to the Thessalonians.

Exploring 2 Thessalonians 3:16

The unknown can be scary and the church at Thessalonica was living in a scary time. They were under persecution and misinformation had circulated that the day of the Lord had already come. This had caused some believers to give up on earning a daily living. These factors were causing problems among the believers and Paul wrote this book to clarify the coming of the Lord and reassure the believers there, to keep living in a way that honored Christ.

In your life, you may have seen what fear does to people and witnessed how quickly gossip spreads and causes problems. As women, it is easy to get caught up in these things and take our eyes off of God. Let me encourage you to read 2 Thessalonians and take to heart Paul's words of comfort and wisdom. No man knows the time of the Lord's return, but as Matthew 24:44 tells us, we are called to be ready.

3:16 Reflect & Connect

The peace of God is a gift that surpasses understanding—a calm assurance rooted in His presence, no matter what we face. In 1 Thessalonians 3:16, Paul reminds us that the Lord Himself is the source of this peace, offering it to us at all times and in every situation. Reflecting on this promise can help us anchor our hearts to Him. Through journaling, we can explore what this peace means in our lives, and creatively express how His presence brings us comfort and strength.

Around the word "PEACE", make a border out of words or phrases that describe what peace feels like or means to you, such as: calm, assurance, God's presence, or rest. Color in the word PEACE and thank God for His peace as you do it.

Peace is sometimes difficult to find in this fallen world. You may be going through a difficult time right now and reading this 3:16 today feels like it doesn't apply to you.

"How can I have peace at all times in every way?"

"Does God know what I am going through?"

"Is it worth continuing to pray when it doesn't seem like God is listening?"

These questions may be part of your life right now. Do not lose hope dear sister, God knows you, He hears you and although it might not seem like it today, He is working everything out for good. What you are asking is not too big for God. He knows your heart and He wants to hear from you. Use this 3:16 when you speak to God about the situation that is causing you a difficult time.

During your Closing Prayer ask God for the peace Paul was talking about, and watch Him begin to move in your life. Peace may happen in an instant, or it may be doled out in small measures of peace which lead to your contentment.

Closing 3:16 Prayer

Heavenly Father,

Just as Paul asked for peace on behalf of the Thessalonians, today I come to You asking for that same peace. I bring my situation to You today and lay it at Your feet, trusting that You will lead me through this time of uncertainty. Lord, I give You the following things in my life ______________________________ and ask for Your wisdom to guide me through.

In Jesus' name I pray,

Amen

1 Timothy 3:16 NLT

Without question, this is the great mystery of our faith. Christ was revealed in a human body and vindicated by the Spirit. He was seen by angels and announced to the nations. He was believed in throughout the world and taken to heaven in glory.

1 Timothy 3:16 NLT

3:16 Biblical Context

Timeline of 1 Timothy 3:1-17

- ✧ **1 Timothy 3:1-7** – Qualification of Elders in the Church.
- ✧ **1 Timothy 3:8-13** – Qualification of Deacons in the Church.
- ✧ **1 Timothy 3:14-15** – Importance of the Church.
- ✧ **1 Timothy 3:16-17** – A hymn of Praise to Jesus.

Exploring 1 Timothy 3:16

This 3:16 is the closing of the first half of the book of 1 Timothy. Paul has shared personally as well as instructed the larger components of the church and he is closing this section with a first century hymn, before shifting to the last 3 chapters of 1 Timothy which dealt with more practical matters of the church. Today's readers will find the words of 1 Timothy give a brief summary of the coming of Jesus.

John 3:16 Correlation: If you examine the phrases in 1 Timothy 3:16, you will find a powerful alignment with phrases found in John 3:16.

HE GAVE HIS ONE AND ONLY SON
JOHN 3:16

Compare to

SO THAT EVERYONE WHO BELIEVES IN HIM WILL NOT PERISH BUT HAVE ETERNAL LIFE.
JOHN 3:16

Compare to

3:16 Reflect & Connect

The book of 1 Timothy is rich with wisdom for life. Many passages in this book give direct advice to women, while others show us how to live and care for those in the church. If you have not read the 6 chapters of 1 Timothy lately, make time to do that this week. Take one chapter a day for the next 6 days and jot down in this journal the things that stand out to you.

Closing 3:16 Prayer

Heavenly Father,

I pray that You will allow time in my life this week to read and comprehend Your word in new ways. Lord, please help me make time to read one chapter of 1 Timothy each day this week. I know there will be things that try to keep me from accomplishing this, so I pray that You will make a way in my life to study what Your word has to say to me this week.

In Jesus' name I pray,

Amen

2 Timothy 3:16 NLT

All Scripture is inspired by God and is useful to teach us what is true and to make us realize what is wrong in our lives. It corrects us when we are wrong and teaches us to do what is right.

2 Timothy 3:16 NLT

3:16 Biblical Context

Timeline of 2 Timothy 3:10-17

- ✧ **2 Timothy 3:10** – Paul reminds Timothy that his (Paul's) life was an open book.
- ✧ **2 Timothy 3:11-12** – Reminder of persecutions Paul had endured and that all believers will experience persecution.
- ✧ **2 Timothy 3:13-15** – While there will be those who seek to do evil, believers should focus on what they have learned from God.
- ✧ **2 Timothy 3:16-17** – Everything learned in scripture is directly from God and useful in a believers life.

Exploring 2 Timothy 3:16

Have you ever thought about the 40+ authors who wrote the Bible? These were people just like you and I. They had days where they were deeply seeking God's will, and other days where they blew it (sometimes in big ways). Either way, they were ordinary people, with all the flaws that come with being human.

If we look at David, who wrote a significant portion of the Psalms, or Moses, who wrote more of the words in the Bible than any other author, we find men who were not perfect, yet God inspired them to write parts of His Word. Just as He did with Paul's letters to Timothy, which God knew would be used in this book for this 3:16, "All Scripture is inspired by God and is useful to teach us what is true and to make us realize what is wrong in our lives. It corrects us when we are wrong and teaches us to do what is right."

Such powerful words to give to the young Timothy, not to mention the rest of us, making it very clear that all Scripture is God breathed to help us live our lives in a way that shows God's love wherever we go and whatever we do.

3:16 Reflect & Connect

As women, we are pulled in many directions and it can feel like we hit the ground running every morning, and then fall exhausted into bed each night. Taking a moment to slow down can seem impossible, or even selfish. Dear sister, God designed His word to give us rest in Him, and this 3:16 is a reminder to take a moment and breathe in His inspired words.

Take a moment and try one or more of these breathing prayers

Names of God Breathing Prayer

- **Breathe in** while thinking a name of God (See list of ***Names/Attributes of God*** found at the end of this journal for ideas)
- **Breathe out** a prayer that corresponds with that name of God

Example:

Breathe in *while thinking the name, Jehovah Jireh (God is our provider)*
Breathe out *by thinking of the ways God provides for you*
Breathe in *while thinking the name, Jehovah Rapha (The Lord is our Healer)*
Breathe out *praising God for specific ways He has healed you or your loved ones.*

Focused Thoughts Breathing Prayer

✦ **Breathe out** a negative emotion

✦ **Breathe in** something positive that involves God and counteracts the negative emotion you breathe out

Example:

Breathe out *stored up anger in your life*

Breathe in *the peace of God*

Breathe out *something you are insecure about*

Breathe in *God standing beside you*

Inhale, Hold, and Exhale Breathing Prayer

✦ Take a deep breath in and hold it. While you are holding your breath, pray over all the people and things that come to your mind. When it is time to release that breath, breathe out thanks to God for hearing you.

Example:

Take a deep breath in and hold it*. Lord please be with Emma as she graduates from college. Please help her to find a job in her chosen field, and help her to make wise choices as she moves forward into the next season of her life.*

Release that breath slowly*. Thank You Lord for hearing my prayer for Emma, as well as the wonderful things that You are going to do in her life.*

BREATHE IN

FAITH

EXHALE DOUBT

Closing 3:16 Prayer

Heavenly Father,

I thank You for being the author of my life. Please help me to live my life in exactly the way You have designed it. Lord, I know that You have breathed life into all of scripture. I ask that You would keep my heart and mind open to what You have for me as I study Your word.

In Jesus' name I pray,

Amen

Hebrews 3:16 NLT

And who was it who rebelled against God, even though they heard His voice? Wasn't it the people Moses led out of Egypt?

Hebrews 3:16 NLT

3:16 Biblical Context

Timeline of Hebrews 3:1-19

- **Hebrews 3:1-5** – Focuses on the superiority of Jesus.
- **Hebrews 3:6** – Christ is in charge of God's house and believers are God's house.
- **Hebrews 3:7-11** – Words of the Holy Spirit (God) about the Israelites testing His patience in the wilderness and being denied entrance to His place of rest.
- **Hebrews 3:12-15** – Warnings for Christians to not make the same mistakes Israel did.
- **Hebrews 3:16-19** reminder of those who rebelled against God and evoked God's anger.

Exploring Hebrews 3:16

The phrases "Monday morning quarterback" or "hindsight is 20/20" are modern-day proverbs, reminding us that when we have all the information, we can make better choices. This is true with Hebrews 3, when we look at the Israelites who followed Moses out of Egypt. They had a promise of things to come, and had heard God's voice, yet they still rebelled, and proceeded to make God angry for the next 40 years. As a result, that entire generation was denied entrance to the promised land.

We know all of that, so we should be able to learn from their mistakes. It should be easy for us to remain faithful and not rebel. Unfortunately, we are flawed humans, and we continue to fall into the same trappings of sin and rebellion.

Yet we must not forget God's grace and love for His people. From the very day that Adam and Eve ate the forbidden fruit, God has worked to regain what was lost that day. Jesus came to restore our relationship with God, fixing what Adam and Eve broke with their disobedience. Now that Jesus has paid the price, those who believe in Him have become a part of God's family.

3:16 Reflect & Connect

We have all been people who have rebelled against God, some of us have done it after we have given our life to Him so this verse may hit hard. Think about the times when you have fallen away, missed the mark and intentionally disobeyed God. Sin always seems fun and harmless at the time you are sinning. The consequences of those sins are tucked away in the recesses of your mind and sometimes we convince ourselves that we are not really doing anything bad, or perhaps not as bad as other people. We often only consider the consequences of sin after we have been caught in that sin.

Now think of the times when you have obeyed God and resisted temptation. Walking with the Lord and following His commandments brings an inner joy and peace to our lives. We do not have to hide from God nor do we dread opening His Word because we find comfort in Him. Comfort that can only be found in a right relationship with God.

Whether you are being nudged by the Holy Spirit to give up a lingering sin or find yourself in a time of closeness with the Lord, write down some of your thoughts about your relationship with God.

As you move to the Closing Prayer, use the prayer prompt to begin your time with God today. If you have the ability to kneel in prayer, consider doing that. Kneeling before your Heavenly Father is one way to focus your mind on God.

Closing 3:16 Prayer

Heavenly Father,

I bow my head in respect to You and thank You for sending Jesus to be my personal Lord and Savior. Lord I come before you now in a time of communication with You. I ask that You will guide this time of prayer.

In Jesus' name I pray,

Amen

James 3:16 NLT

For wherever there is jealousy and selfish ambition, there you will find disorder and evil of every kind.
James 3:16 NLT

3:16 Biblical Context

Timeline of James 3:1-18

- **James 3:1-8** – James focuses on two things; the damage the tongue can do if not reigned in, and mastery of the tongue as the beginning of spiritual maturity.
- **James 3:9-15** – James demonstrates how the tongue can cause a person to be on both ends of the spectrum of human experiences.
- **James 3:16-18** – James shows the difference between those who are truly wise in the Lord and those who are relying on worldly wisdom.

Exploring James 3:16

James wrote to the early Christians, instructing them on how to tame their tongues, and focus on becoming mature believers. He lists many examples of how the tongue can derail us. Though such a small part of the body, James compares it to the bit of a horse, or the rudder of a ship, which can steer those large and powerful creations where it leads them.

This 3:16 uses the words, jealousy, selfishness, disorder and evil of every kind. These words can be linked to the tongue and are a stern reminder that if we don't control our tongues, we can set the forest ablaze with our words.

The beauty of it is that, 3:17-18, tells us if we heed God's wisdom, and learn to tame our tongues, we can become peacemakers instead of leaving destruction in our wake. We can be the type of women who plant seeds of peace wherever we go, and reap a harvest of righteousness.

3:16 Reflect & Connect

As you learned while exploring this 3:16, jealousy and selfish ambition can thrive, and these are things that women often struggle with. Being jealous of what another woman has or looks like is a poison that can eat up our lives. It can lead to gossip and division and can ultimately cause you to grow further and further away from God.

Our Creator, calls us to a higher standard—to seek wisdom that is pure, peace-loving, gentle, and full of mercy. As women, we are uniquely positioned to sow seeds of peace, creating harmony in our relationships and environments. When we choose to be peacemakers, we reflect God's heart and invite His blessing into our lives.

In the area provided, write **"Wisdom Garden"** at the top, then draw or use stickers to create a garden with at least 8 different plants, leaving room at the bottom to write.

Label each plant with a quality from James 3:17 (pure, peace loving, gentle, agreeable, merciful, good deeds, impartial, sincere).

In the soil beneath the plants, write practical ways you can "cultivate" these qualities in your life this week.

Closing 3:16 Prayer

Heavenly Father,

Thank You for the wisdom You so freely offer. I come before You knowing that there have been times I've let jealousy or selfish ambition take root in my heart. I pray that You will give me a generous spirit to serve Your people. Lord, I want to reconnect with You now, please fill me with Your peace, the kind that is pure, gentle, and full of mercy. I will lean on You to help me reflect Your love in the way I speak, act and think, especially when conflict arises.

In Jesus' name I pray,

Amen

1 Peter 3:16 NLT

But do this in a gentle and respectful way. Keep your conscience clear. Then if people speak against you, they will be ashamed when they see what a good life you live because you belong to Christ.

1 Peter 3:16 NLT

3:16 Reflect & Connect

Timeline of 1 Peter 3:8-18

- **1 Peter 3:8-12** – These verses remind us how God has called us to behave to our brothers and sisters. Verse 10 has very similar wording to Psalm 34:12 stating to keep your tongue from evil and your lips from speaking lies.
- **1 Peter 3:13-17** – Reminder that God rewards those who suffer for doing good. Explain the hope you have with others.
- **1 Peter 3:18** – Look at how Christ, who did not sin, suffered and died for our sins and was raised to life again.

Exploring 1 Peter 3:16

Suffering for doing what is right is a consistent theme in 1 Peter, it is written about in every chapter and always includes how these trials are a part of every believer's journey in this world. This 3:16 speaks about people speaking bad about you who will be put to shame when they see your good life as a believer of Christ. 1:6 speaks of various trials that believers will go through then tells us to rejoice as they are temporary. 2:21 speaks on unjust rulers and how we are to silence evil by doing good. 4:2 talks about suffering for resisting carnal desires will increase our determination in these situations. 4:13-14 speaks about religious persecution allowing us to partake in Christ's suffering. 4:19 speaks about suffering for spiritual growth allows us to commit our lives to the Lord.

1 Peter 3:16 offers a compelling reminder to women of faith to live with integrity and grace, even when facing challenges. Encouraging us to keep our conscience clear by living in a way that honors Christ, so that when others speak against us, our good behavior will prove them wrong. This 3:16, nestled in a passage about unity, kindness, and enduring suffering for doing good, reminds us that our lives are a reflection of Christ's love and truth.

As women, we often face moments where our faith is tested, but this is also where our testimony shines the brightest. By responding to criticism or hardship with gentleness, humility, and unwavering hope, we not only glorify God, but also open the door for others to see Him in us. 1 Peter 3:15 challenges us to embrace every opportunity to share our faith—whether through our words or actions.

Let verses 15 & 16 encourage you to live boldly and gracefully, always ready to share Christ's love with others. Your testimony, lived out and spoken with kindness, is a powerful tool to draw others closer to Him.

Something to Think About

1 Peter 3:16 reminds us

that our actions

speak louder

than accusations.

Are you living in a way that reflects Christ's goodness, even when criticized?

3:16 Reflect & Connect

Testimony time.
1 minute testimony
3 minute testimony
Conversational testimony.
Use the space to write down a one minute version of what God has done in your life since you came to know Him.

Now write down a bit longer version, 3 minutes, including how you came to realize that you needed God, what has happened in your life after you Gave your life to Him.

Now practice your 1 minute & 3 minute testimonies until they come easily without looking at this journal. You may want to take a picture of what you have written and keep it with you, and be able to access it when you need it to practice, to use, or as a reminder.

Be Ready to Share Christ

Once you're done with those, take some time to work on a longer version of your testimony. Think of questions that someone might ask you, and how you would answer them while you try and keep the conversation moving toward Jesus.

If you have a close Christian friend, offer to take her to lunch and let her know you are going to practice sharing your testimony with her.

Live Boldly and Gracefully

Closing 3:16 Prayer

Heavenly Father,

I am thankful for the testimony You have given me. My testimony is very personal and I ask that You give me the courage to share my testimony with someone so that they have the opportunity to come to know You as I do. Lord, now that I have written my testimony, Give me the boldness to seek out opportunities to share my faith.

In Jesus's name I pray,

Amen

2 Peter 3:16 NLT

Speaking of these things in all of his (Paul's) letters. Some of his comments are hard to understand, and those who are ignorant and unstable have twisted his letters to mean something quite different, just as they do with other parts of Scripture. And this will result in their destruction.

2 Peter 3:16 NLT

3:16 Biblical Context

Timeline of 2 Peter 3:8-18

- ✧ **2 Peter 3:8-9** – These verses explain the Lord's coming is not slow but rather patient so others can come to Him.
- ✧ **2 Peter 3:10-13** – Description of what the Lord's return will look like.
- ✧ **2 Peter 3:14-16** – Reminders for Christians while we wait for the Lord's return and what happens to those who twist Scripture here on earth.
- ✧ **2 Peter 3:17-18** – Final reminder to not fall away, but to grow in grace while we wait on the Lord to return.

Exploring 2 Peter 3:16

In 2 Peter, Peter speaks of 4 important topics of a Christian's life:

- ✦ Growing in faith
- ✦ Paying attention to the scriptures
- ✦ The danger of false teachings
- ✦ The return of the Lord

What a power packed book in 3 short chapters. This is a guidebook for the Christian faith which reminds believers to be wary of false teachings, as well as the importance of growing spiritually.

Each person must accept the Lord's free gift of Salvation on their own just as each person must grow in their faith on their own. You can not rely on the fact that your grandmother was a Christian, you must make those decisions for yourself.

In this 3:16, the author acknowledges that some of Paul's writings are "hard to understand" and warns that those who are "ignorant and unstable" twist these teachings to their own destruction. This statement carries two important truths: first, Peter affirms that Paul's letters are part of the inspired Word of God. Second, it highlights the danger of misinterpreting or distorting biblical teachings, which can lead people away from God's truth.

As women studying the Bible, this verse encourages us to approach Scripture with humility and a heart ready to listen, relying on God's Spirit to bring understanding. This passage also challenges us to persevere in studying God's Word, even when it's puzzling, trusting that understanding will come as we seek Him with open hearts and minds.

3:16 Reflect & Connect

Here is another reminder to read scripture in the context of the verses and passages around it. When we pair this 3:16 with 3:15 NLT, *"And remember, our Lord's patience gives people time to be saved. This is what our beloved brother Paul also wrote to you with the wisdom God gave him."* We find that it gives us more clarity. When we widen that view even more and read all that 2 Peter has to share, we come away with a deeper understanding of what God expects of believers.

As we learned in this 3:16, Scripture is often puzzling, but the more you study God's Word, the more the pieces start fitting together into a beautiful and clear picture of God's truth. While some passages may seem hard to understand, they are not meant to confuse or frustrate us. Instead, seek God's wisdom and grow deeper in our understanding of His Word.

Using the puzzle outline provided here, write one concept or phrase inside each puzzle piece that is inspired by 2 Peter 3:16-18.

Example:

"God's Word is trustworthy" or "Grow in grace and knowledge"

God's Truth Fits Together Perfectly

Closing 3:16 Prayer

Heavenly Father,

You have gifted me with the ability to study Your word and learn how Your word applies to my life. God I read in Your word that ______________________________, and I ask that You give me further clarity on how I can apply this to my walk with You.

In Jesus' name I pray,

Amen

1 John 3:16 NLT

We know what real love is because Jesus gave up His life for us. So we also ought to give up our lives for our brothers and sisters.

1 John 3:16 NLT

3:16 Biblical Context

Timeline of 1 John 3:11-24

- **1 John 3:11-15** – Reminds us of the evil committed by Cain. This warning serves to remind us that Christians should love one another, and not be surprised when the world hates us for the love that we have in Christ.
- **1 John 3:16** – Follow the example of Christ who loved us and went to the cross to show us how we should love our brothers and sisters.
- **1 John 3:17-24** – Reminders to love others with our actions, not let our hearts lose sight of Gods' love, and to know the Spirit He has given to all who believe in Him.

Exploring 1 John 3:16

Just reading this 3:16 immediately brings to mind the most well known 3:16 in the Bible, John 3:16. That could be because John and 1 John are commonly believed to be written by the same person. John, Jesus' Disciple, who is also thought to have authored all of the books with the title John as well as Revelation. These 5 books were most likely written in the order they appear in the Bible, later in John's life. God inspired John to write and as we see the correlation between John 3:16 and 1 John 3:16, it becomes clear that it was important to God that we as believers keep these verses in mind.

John 3:16 Correlation: Is all about love expressed by sacrifice. The word love in 1 John 3:16 means sacrificial love. This is the same wording used in John 3:16 to describe the sacrifice Jesus made for us on the cross. 1 John 3:16 goes on to remind Christians to show that same sacrificial love to those around us. Both verses emphasize that true love is selfless and willing to sacrifice for the good of others. John wanted to emphasize that love is an integral part of our faith.

3:16 Reflect & Connect

This verse is as close to John 3:16 as we have. Write John 3:16 and 1 John 3:16 on the lines below and meditate on how these verses apply to your life. The last sentence of 1 John 3:16 may bring to mind those brothers and sisters in your life who support you and build you up in your faith. Write their names along the bottom of this page as a reminder to pray for those whom God has placed in our lives.

God's love is the ultimate example of sacrifice--Jesus gave His life so we could live. In 1 John 3:16, we are reminded that true love is not just words, but actions, often requiring selflessness and service to others. As women of faith, we are called to reflect this sacrificial love in our daily lives, sharing God's love through kindness, compassion, and grace.

Fill the Cross with Acts of Sacrificial Love: Inside the cross provided, write small acts of sacrificial love you can do this week, such as: *"help a neighbor", "pray for someone who's hurt me", "encourage someone you don't know well"* or *"volunteer at church"*. Fill the cross with your actions, leaving no empty space.

Pray Over Your Commitments: Spend time during your Closing Prayer praying over what you've written. Take a picture of the cross as a visible reminder of your calling to love as Jesus loved.

Closing 3:16 Prayer

Heavenly Father,

Thank you for Jesus willingness to sacrifice His life for the world. I ask that You give me a heart for others. I lift my list of people up to You in prayer.

In Jesus's name I pray,
Amen

Revelation 3:16 NLT

But since you are like lukewarm water, neither hot nor cold, I will spit you out of my mouth!

Revelation 3:16 NLT

3:16 Biblical Context

Timeline of Revelation 2:1-3:21

- **Revelation 2:1- 3:13** – John gives prophecy messages to 6 churches.
- **Revelation 3:14** – Jesus calls himself the one who is the Amen, the faithful and true witness, the beginning of God's new creation.
- **Revelation 3:15-16** – Being hot or cold would be better than lukewarm- the church at Laodicea was complacent, smug, and self reliant.
- **Revelation 3:17-18** – Laodicea sees themselves as rich and having no need for God.
- **Revelation 3:19-21** – Jesus is giving Laodicea a chance to understand their need is not for material wealth but for the true spiritual wealth that comes only from Christ.

Exploring Revelation 3:16

A unique message was sent to the churches in 7 different cities

Ephesus - Praised for their good work and discipline to church teachings. Reprimanded for losing their first love

Smyrna - Praised for being a church that stood up under suffering. Not reprimanded for anything.

Pergamum - Praised for standing faithful in a city corrupt with sin. Reprimanded for allowing the world to compromise the church.

Thyatira - Praised for its love, faith, service and patience. Reprimanded for allowing immorality and fake teachings.

Sardis - Not praised for anything. Reprimanded for being Christians in name only.

Philadelphia - God praised this church for their four strengths. They had an open door, strength, kept God's word, and had not denied Him. There were no reprimands.

Laodicea- Not praised for anything. Reprimanded for being lukewarm and found them lacking in every way.

The final verse in this Bible study journal is part of the final letter to the 7 churches. John is speaking to Laodicea because they have become lukewarm to sharing the Gospel, and to their need for God, as their wealth had made them full of self-sufficiency and complacency.

This 3:16 gives believers a strong warning to guard against becoming lukewarm. John impresses on us how being lukewarm is a dangerous place to be, as the Laodicean's are completely blind to what is wrong in their lives. So commit yourself to turning up the heat! Don't let yourself get complacent, seek God in all that you do. Take a stand for Christ and step out boldly in your faith. Use the testimony you have written in 1 Peter 3:16 to help guide you as you stay on fire for the Lord, living a life filled with serving God and sharing the gospel with others.

3:16 Reflect & Connect

Write down 1 way you can be bold in your faith, 1 way you can fight complacency, and 1 way you will rely on God. Look back through this journal at the things you doodled or journaled. Read through the prayers that you wrote and use them to keep yourself from becoming a complacent Christian. Step out today and live the life that Christ has called you. Carry the 3:16's of the Bible with you .

I can be bold in my faith by ______________________________

____

I can fight complacency by ____

____

I will rely on God by ____

____

Closing 3:16 Prayer

Heavenly Father,

Thank You for guiding me through Your Word. I pray that You will take what I have learned in this Bible journal and use it to strengthen my relationship with You. God I come to You now with the following things on my mind ____________________, I thank You for hearing me and for working in my life.

In Jesus's name I pray,

Amen

Names/Attributes of God

Below is a list of names for God found in the Bible. Each name is accompanied by its meaning and at least one verse reference. They are listed in alphabetical order for convenience.

1. **Abba** – Father

   Reference: Romans 8:15, Galatians 4:6

   Meaning: This name conveys intimacy and closeness, showing God as a loving and caring Father who invites His children to approach Him with confidence.

2. **Adonai** – Lord, Master

   Reference: Psalm 8:1, Isaiah 6:1

   Meaning: This title expresses God's sovereign authority and rightful ownership over all creation. It reflects submission to His lordship.

3. **El Elyon** – The Most High God

   Reference: Genesis 14:18-20, Psalm 57:2

   Meaning: This name shows God's supreme authority over all creation and His exalted position above every other power or deity.

4. **El Shaddai** – God Almighty

Reference: Genesis 17:1, Psalm 91:1

Meaning: This name reveals God's all-sufficient nature, His power to nurture, and His ability to bless abundantly. It is often associated with His covenant promises.

5. **Elohim** – God, Creator

Reference: Genesis 1:1, Deuteronomy 10:17

Meaning: This plural form of the Hebrew word *Eloah* (God or deity) emphasizes God's majesty and power as the Creator of the heavens and the earth.

6. **Immanuel** – God with us

Reference: Isaiah 7:14, Matthew 1:23

Meaning: This name signifies God's presence with His people, fulfilled through the incarnation of Jesus Christ.

7. **Jehovah Jireh** – The Lord will provide

Reference: Genesis 22:14, Philippians 4:19

Meaning: This name was declared by Abraham after God provided a ram for sacrifice instead of his son, Isaac. It emphasizes God's provision in times of need.

8. **Jehovah Nissi** – The Lord is my banner

Reference: Exodus 17:15, Psalm 60:4

Meaning: After the Israelites' victory over the Amalekites, Moses built an altar and called it Jehovah Nissi, signifying that God leads and fights for His people.

9. **Jehovah Rapha** – The God who heals

   Reference: Exodus 15:26, Psalm 103:3

   Meaning: This name reflects God's power to restore physical, emotional, and spiritual health. He is the ultimate healer who mends brokenness and brings wholeness.

10. **Jehovah Shalom** – The Lord is peace

   Reference: Judges 6:24, Isaiah 9:6

   Meaning: Gideon used this name for God after being assured of peace despite facing overwhelming challenges. It signifies God's presence bringing calm and wholeness.

11. **Jehovah Tsidkenu** – The Lord our righteousness

   Reference: Jeremiah 23:6, 2 Corinthians 5:21

   Meaning: This name points to God's role in providing righteousness to His people, particularly through the coming of the Messiah, who justifies and sanctifies.

12. **Yahweh** – I AM

   Reference: Exodus 3:14, John 8:58

   Meaning: This name signifies God's eternal existence and self-sufficiency. It reveals Him as the unchanging and ever-present God.

Ways to Use this 3:16 Bible Study Journal

This 3:16 Bible Study Journal can be used in several different ways as both a Personal Bible Study and/or a Group Bible Study. Over the next few pages you will find guides for four different ways to complete this study. Choose the way that works best for your Personal or Group Bible Study, or use one of the suggestions as a template to make a Bible Study plan that works for you or your group.

✦ **6 Week Cluster Bible Study** - Complete 8-9 Chapters of 3:16 per week
✦ **8 Week Daily Bible Study** - Complete 1 Chapter each day (6 per week)
✦ **12 Week Bible Study** – Complete 4 Chapters each week
✦ **52 Week Bible Study** – Complete 1 Chapter per week, with 3 vacation weeks built in.

Helpful Hints:

- ✧ Use the checkboxes to keep yourself on track as you complete each chapter.
- ✧ Give yourself grace. If you fall behind, don't give up. Start where you left off at your first opportunity.
- ✧ It takes time to get in the habit of studying your Bible, so set an alarm on your phone to remind you when it's time to open up 3:16.
- ✧ To minimize distractions during your Personal Bible Study time, choose a place that is quiet and has the least amount of interruptions possible.
- ✧ Have a designated Bible Study tote bag in which you store all of your Bible Study materials, such as: pens, pencils, highlighters, colored pencils, stickers, etc., along with your Bible and Bible Study book (3:16). Whether personal or group, this will simplify your Bible Study time when your supplies are grab and go.
- ✧ Settle your heart and mind in the right place before you start your Bible study, pray before you begin Your time with God.

6 Week Cluster Bible Study

This is the most intensive plan of the four guides provided as it will require you and/or your group to complete 8-9 chapters every week.

- ❑ **Week 1**
- ❑ Genesis 3:16
- ❑ Exodus 3:16
- ❑ Leviticus 3:16
- ❑ Numbers 3:16
- ❑ Deuteronomy 3:16
- ❑ Joshua 3:16
- ❑ Judges 3:16
- ❑ Ruth 3:16

- ❑ **Week 2**
- ❑ 1 Samuel 3:16
- ❑ 2 Samuel 3:16
- ❑ 1 Kings 3:16
- ❑ 2 Kings 3:16
- ❑ 1 Chronicles 3:16
- ❑ 2 Chronicles 3:16
- ❑ Nehemiah 3:16
- ❑ Job 3:16

- ❑ **Week 3**
- ❑ Proverbs 3:16
- ❑ Ecclesiastes 3:16
- ❑ Isaiah 3:16
- ❑ Jeremiah 3:16
- ❑ Lamentations 3:16
- ❑ Ezekiel 3:16
- ❑ Daniel 3:16
- ❑ Joel 3:16

- ❑ **Week 4**
- ❑ Nahum 3:16
- ❑ Habakkuk 3:16
- ❑ Zephaniah 3:16
- ❑ Malachi 3:16
- ❑ Matthew 3:16
- ❑ Mark 3:16
- ❑ Luke 3:16
- ❑ John 3:16

- ❑ **Week 5**
- ❑ Acts 3:16
- ❑ Romans 3:16
- ❑ 1 Corinthians 3:16
- ❑ 2 Corinthians 3:16
- ❑ Galatians 3:16
- ❑ Ephesians 3:16
- ❑ Philippians 3:16
- ❑ Colossians 3:16

- ❑ **Week 6**
- ❑ 2 Thessalonians 3:16
- ❑ 1 Timothy 3:16
- ❑ 2 Timothy 3:16
- ❑ Hebrews 3:16
- ❑ James 3:16
- ❑ 1 Peter 3:16
- ❑ 2 Peter 3:16
- ❑ 1 John 3:16
- ❑ Revelation 3:16

8 Week Daily Study

This plan sets a steady pace, as you and/or your group are required to do 1 Chapter per day (6 Chapters per week & 1 day of rest).

- ❑ Day 1 - Genesis 3:16
- ❑ Day 2 - Exodus 3:16
- ❑ Day 3 - Leviticus 3:16
- ❑ Day 4 - Numbers 3:16
- ❑ Day 5 - Deuteronomy 3:16
- ❑ Day 6 - Joshua 3:16
- ❑ Day 7 - Judges 3:16
- ❑ Day 8 - Ruth 3:16
- ❑ Day 9 - 1 Samuel 3:16
- ❑ Day 10 - 2 Samuel 3:16
- ❑ Day 11 - 1 Kings 3:16
- ❑ Day 12 - 2 Kings 3:16
- ❑ Day 13 - 1 Chronicles 3:16
- ❑ Day 14 - 2 Chronicles 3:16
- ❑ Day 15 - Nehemiah 3:16
- ❑ Day 16 - Job 3:16
- ❑ Day 17 - Proverbs 3:16
- ❑ Day 18 - Ecclesiastes 3:16
- ❑ Day 19 - Isaiah 3:16
- ❑ Day 20 - Jeremiah 3:16
- ❑ Day 21 - Lamentations 3:16
- ❑ Day 22 - Ezekiel 3:16
- ❑ Day 23 - Daniel 3:16
- ❑ Day 24 - Joel 3:16
- ❑ Day 25 - Nahum 3:16
- ❑ Day 26 - Habakkuk 3:16
- ❑ Day 27 - Zephaniah 3:16
- ❑ Day 28 - Malachi 3:16
- ❑ Day 29 - Matthew 3:16
- ❑ Day 30 - Mark 3:16
- ❑ Day 31 - Luke 3:16
- ❑ Day 32 - John 3:16
- ❑ Day 33 - Acts 3:16
- ❑ Day 34 - Romans 3:16
- ❑ Day 35 - 1 Corinthians 3:16
- ❑ Day 36 - 2 Corinthians 3:16
- ❑ Day 37 - Galatians 3:16
- ❑ Day 38 - Ephesians 3:16
- ❑ Day 39 - Philippians 3:16
- ❑ Day 40 - Colossians 3:16
- ❑ Day 41 - 2 Thessalonians 3:16
- ❑ Day 42 - 1 Timothy 3:16
- ❑ Day 43 - 2 Timothy 3:16
- ❑ Day 44 - Hebrews 3:16
- ❑ Day 45 - James 3:16
- ❑ Day 46 - 1 Peter 3:16
- ❑ Day 47 - 2 Peter 3:16
- ❑ Day 48 - 1 John 3:16
- ❑ Day 49 - Revelation 3:16

12 Week Bible Study

This schedule is the best paced Bible Study for weekly Group Studies, though it may also be used as a personal study for those with busier lives.

❑ **Week 1**
❑ Genesis 3:16
❑ Exodus 3:16
❑ Leviticus 3:16
❑ Numbers 3:16

❑ **Week 2**
❑ Deuteronomy 3:16
❑ Joshua 3:16
❑ Judges 3:16
❑ Ruth 3:16

❑ **Week 3**
❑ 1 Samuel 3:16
❑ 2 Samuel 3:16
❑ 1 Kings 3:16
❑ 2 Kings 3:16

❑ **Week 4**
❑ 1 Chronicles 3:16
❑ 2 Chronicles 3:16
❑ Nehemiah 3:16
❑ Job 3:16

❑ **Week 5**
❑ Proverbs 3:16
❑ Ecclesiastes 3:16
❑ Isaiah 3:16
❑ Jeremiah 3:16

❑ **Week 6**
❑ Lamentations 3:16
❑ Ezekiel 3:16
❑ Daniel 3:16
❑ Joel 3:16

❑ **Week 7**
❑ Nahum 3:16
❑ Habakkuk 3:16
❑ Zephaniah 3:16
❑ Malachi 3:16

❑ **Week 8**
❑ Matthew 3:16
❑ Mark 3:16
❑ Luke 3:16
❑ John 3:16

❑ **Week 9**
❑ Acts 3:16
❑ Romans 3:16
❑ 1 Corinthians 3:16
❑ 2 Corinthians 3:16

❑ **Week 10**
❑ Galatians 3:16
❑ Ephesians 3:16
❑ Philippians 3:16
❑ Colossians 3:16

❑ **Week 11**
❑ 2 Thessalonians 3:16
❑ 1 Timothy 3:16
❑ Leviticus 3:16
❑ Hebrews 3:16

❑ **Week 12**
❑ James 3:16
❑ 1 Peter 3:16
❑ 2 Peter 3:16
❑ 1 John 3:16 & ❑ Revelation 3:16

52 Week Bible Study

This plan allows you or a group to really dig into each chapter as it only requires the completion of 1 chapter per week. This schedule is meant to be completed in one year, so there are three built in vacation weeks that you can take any time throughout the year.

- ❑ Week 1 - Genesis 3:16
- ❑ Week 2 - Exodus 3:16
- ❑ Week 3 - Leviticus 3:16
- ❑ Week 4 - Numbers 3:16
- ❑ Week 5 - Deuteronomy 3:16
- ❑ Week 6 - Joshua 3:16
- ❑ Week 7 - Judges 3:16
- ❑ Week 8 - Ruth 3:16
- ❑ Week 9 - 1 Samuel 3:16
- ❑ Week 10 - 2 Samuel 3:16
- ❑ Week 11 - 1 Kings 3:16
- ❑ Week 12 - 2 Kings 3:16
- ❑ Week 13 - 1 Chronicles 3:16
- ❑ Week 14 - 2 Chronicles 3:16
- ❑ Week 15 - Nehemiah 3:16
- ❑ Week 16 - Job 3:16
- ❑ Week 17 - Proverbs 3:16
- ❑ Week 18 - Ecclesiastes 3:16
- ❑ Week 19 - Isaiah 3:16
- ❑ Week 20 - Jeremiah 3:16
- ❑ Week 21 - Lamentations 3:16
- ❑ Week 22 - Ezekiel 3:16
- ❑ Week 23 - Daniel 3:16
- ❑ Week 24 - Joel 3:16
- ❑ Week 25 - Nahum 3:16
- ❑ Week 26 - Habakkuk 3:16
- ❑ Week 27 - Zephaniah 3:16
- ❑ Week 28 - Malachi 3:16
- ❑ Week 29 - Matthew 3:16
- ❑ Week 30 - Mark 3:16
- ❑ Week 31 - Luke 3:16
- ❑ Week 32 - John 3:16
- ❑ Week 33 - Acts 3:16
- ❑ Week 34 - Romans 3:16
- ❑ Week 35 - 1 Corinthians 3:16
- ❑ Week 36 - 2 Corinthians 3:16
- ❑ Week 37 - Galatians 3:16
- ❑ Week 38 - Ephesians 3:16
- ❑ Week 39 - Philippians 3:16
- ❑ Week 40 - Colossians 3:16
- ❑ Week 41- 2 Thessalonians 3:16
- ❑ Week 42 - 1 Timothy 3:16
- ❑ Week 43 - 2 Timothy 3:16
- ❑ Week 44 - Hebrews 3:16
- ❑ Week 45 - James 3:16
- ❑ Week 46 - 1 Peter 3:16
- ❑ Week 47 - 2 Peter 3:16
- ❑ Week 48 - 1 John 3:16
- ❑ Week 49 - Revelation 3:16
- ❑ Week 50 - ________________
- ❑ Week 51 - ________________
- ❑ Week 52 - ________________

Prayer of Salvation

"Look! I stand at the door and knock. If you hear My voice and open the door, I will come in..."
Revelation 3:20a NLT

Heavenly Father,

I realize that I have done things that do not please You, and those sins have separated me from You. I ask that You forgive me for my sins and make me clean in Your sight. Jesus, please come into my life as my Lord and Savior. I accept Your free gift of eternal life and I will do my best to live for You all the days of my life.

In Jesus' name I pray,

Amen

About the Author

Jennifer Galvan's formative years were spent in a small town in Middle Tennessee. Shortly after graduating from the University of Tennessee, she packed her southern accent and a love for writing and moved to Orange County, California. She and her husband have raised 2 biological children and served as a host family to International students. She has dedicated her career to working with children who have been affected by childhood abuse and trauma and continues to work full time with youth in the foster care system. Her ministry as a pastor's wife began when she was 29 years old and continues on today where her husband serves as the Senior Pastor of their church. Jennifer has a passion for connecting with God's word through Bible journaling which can be found in her debut book *Citrus Sisterhood*. She is currently working on additional Bible journaling projects. Connect with Jennifer at https://jengalvan.com or at https://galvanbooks.com

message that no force can stand against Him. This section serves as a reminder that the same God who acted powerfully in the past remains faithful and will act again to deliver and restore His people.

This 3:16 shifts this song of prayer to Habakkuk's personal response. The prophet trembles with fear and awe at the vision of God's judgment and timing. He expresses a willingness to wait patiently, even as disaster approaches. This leads Habakkuk to declare his faith despite his fear and find strength in God alone.

> "Yet I will rejoice in the Lord! I will be joyful in the God of my salvation! And The Sovereign Lord is my strength. He makes me as surefooted as a deer, able to tread upon the heights."
> Habakkuk 3:18-19 NLT

3:16 Reflect & Connect

Reflect on some of the words or phrases in Habakkuk 3:16-19 that speak to you.

> [16] *I trembled inside when I heard this; my lips quivered with fear. My legs gave way beneath me, and I shook in terror. I will wait quietly for the coming day when disaster will strike the people who invade us.*[17] *Even though the fig trees have no blossoms, and there are no grapes on the vines; even though the olive crop fails, and the fields lie empty and barren; even though the flocks die in the fields, and the cattle barns are empty,*[18] *yet I will rejoice in the Lord! I will be joyful in the God of my salvation!*[19] *The Sovereign Lord is my strength! He makes me as surefooted as a deer, able to tread upon the heights.*
> Habakkuk 3:16-19 NLT

Use the lines provided to pour out your praise to God for His Holiness, Might and Power.

Habakkuk 3:16 NLT

I trembled inside when I heard this; my lips quivered with fear. My legs gave way beneath me, and I shook in terror. I will wait quietly for the coming day when disaster will strike the people who invade us.

Habakkuk 3:16 NLT

3:16 Biblical Context

Timeline of Habakkuk 3:1-19

✧ **Habakkuk 3:1-2** – Habakkuk's prayer for revival.
✧ **Habakkuk 3:3-15** – Habakkuk's vision of God's power.
✧ **Habakkuk 3:16-19** – Habakkuk's response of fear and faith.

Exploring Habakkuk 3:16

Habakkuk 3 is a powerful chapter where the prophet transitions from questioning God, to embracing the task God has assigned him to do.

This chapter begins with a prayer in which Habakkuk acknowledges God's mighty works throughout history and pleads for Him to revive them in Habakkuk's time. Habakkuk, although scared, trusts in the Lord even when he can't see the outcome. Finally, Habakkuk sings his prayer, acknowledging God as a mighty warrior and sovereign Lord. This final prayer reflects a deep understanding that God's plans are far greater than human comprehension, and that His mercy is always present, even in the midst of discipline.

Verses 3-15 provide a poetic and vivid depiction of God's majestic power. Drawing from Israel's history, Habakkuk recalls events like the Exodus as well as God's deliverance of His people. The imagery of nature trembling before God, highlights His dominion over all creation, reinforcing the